The
Bulldog

An Owner's Guide To

A HAPPY HEALTHY PET

Howell Book House

Howell Book House
A Simon & Schuster Macmillan Company
1633 Broadway
New York, NY 10019

Macmillan Publishing books may be purchased for business or sales promotional use. For information please write: Special Markets Department, Macmillan Publishing USA, 1633 Broadway, New York, NY 10019.

Library of Congress Cataloging-in-Publication Data
Andrée, Marie.
The bulldog: an owner's guide to a happy, healthy pet / Marie Andrée.
p. cm.

ISBN 0-87605-432-7

1. Bulldogs.   I. Title.   II. Series.
SF429.B85A54   1997
636.72—dc21   97-35869
                      CIP

Manufactured in the United States of America
10 9 8 7 6 5 4 3 2 1

Series Director: Amanda Pisani
Series Assistant Director: Jennifer Liberts
Book Design by Michele Laseau
Cover Design by Iris Jeromnimon
Illustration: Laura Robbins
Photography:
  Cover by Renée Stockdale
  Marie Andrée: 27, 29
  Joan Balzarini: 37
  Paulette Braun: 42–43, 44, 46, 73
  Betty Fischer: 25, 26
  Howell Book House: 16, 18, 19
  Renée Stockdale: i, 2–3, 5, 12, 13, 14, 32, 35, 36, 51, 54, 56, 58, 60, 65, 66, 67, 68, 70, 71, 75, 84, 92
  Judith Strom: 10, 64, 76
  Faith Uridel: 7, 49
Production Team: Stephanie Hammett, Clint Lahnen, Stephanie Mohler, Dennis Sheehan, Terri Sheehan

Contents

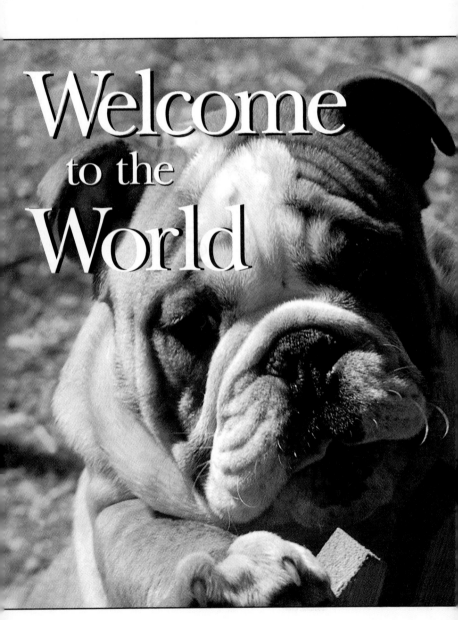

Welcome
to the
World

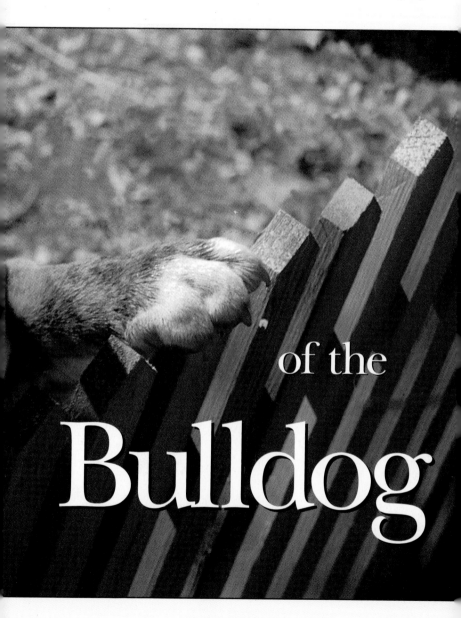

of the

Bulldog

External Features of the Bulldog

chapter 1

What Is a Bulldog?

God summoned a beast from the field and He said, "Behold man, created in my image. Therefore adore him. You shall protect him in the wilderness, shepherd his flocks, watch over his children, accompany him wherever he may go—even unto civilization. You shall be his ally, his slave and his companion.

"To do these things," God said, "I endow you with these instincts uncommon to other beasts: faithfulness, devotion and understanding surpassing those of man himself. Lest it impair your loyalty, you shall be blind to the faults of man. Lest it impair your understanding,

5

you are denied the power of words. Let no fault of language cleave an accord beyond that of man with any other beast or even man with man. Speak to your master only with your mind and through honest eyes.

"Walk by his side, sleep in his doorway, forage for him, ward off his enemies, carry his burdens, share his afflictions, love him and comfort him. And in return for this, man will fulfill your needs and wants, which shall be only food, shelter and affection.

"So be silent, and be a friend to man. Guide him through the perils along the way to the land that I have promised him. This shall be your destiny and your immortality." So spake the Lord. And the bulldog heard and was content.

—from Genesis

A Bulldog is a symbol of tenacity, courage and strength. If given half a chance, he will be one of the best friends you will ever have. He accepts you as you are, whether you are a success or a failure, happy or sad, lazy or energetic, young or old. And you, in turn, accept him for how he comes to you. His ears are not cropped nor is his tail docked. His coat is smooth and is not trimmed into fancy shapes.

Introduction to the Standard

As every breed recognized by the American Kennel Club has a standard or blueprint that describes its perfect dog, so does the Bulldog.

The Bulldog standard was adopted in 1896 and few changes in the wording have been made in over 100 years. In spite of this, the Bulldog of today does not look like the Bulldog of 1896.

INTERPRETING THE STANDARD

It could be that today's fanciers, breeders and judges have a different interpretation of the meaning of the words written long ago. Another possibility is that physical differences are due to the better medical care and nutrition available to Bulldogs today. A cesarean section is a relatively safe procedure today, so live puppies with heavier shoulders and bigger heads are possible. This sturdy physique is what the standard calls for, but when is heavy too heavy and when is a big head too big? These issues should not pose a problem because the dog is supposed to be balanced—her head and shoulders must be proportionate to the ideal weight of the dog. The standard calls for a medium sized (about 50 to 55 pounds) dog, but what is "about"? Some people consider 60 pounds to fall in that range.

The Bulldog is a symbol of courage and tenacity.

Another change that has come about is the name of the breed. For many years the Bulldog was known as the English Bulldog, but several years ago English was dropped and now this breed is known simply as the Bulldog.

WHY DO WE HAVE A STANDARD?

Because different people think of the Bulldog in different ways, it is necessary that a pattern or standard be developed and adhered to. If there were no standard, one person who believes that a "real" Bulldog has to be 80 pounds and white would argue with the next person who feels that a "real" Bulldog must have a fighting or aggressive disposition. If these people bred Bulldogs with their different ideals in mind, there would be no Bulldogs in a few short years. We would just have a mish mosh of dogs with differing sizes and dispositions.

It is difficult to always get dogs that fit the standard. But honest, serious breeders keep trying to eliminate genetic faults that will impair the health and life of a dog. All serious breeders hope to break even financially, but their first priority is a healthy, happy animal. We all want to win in the showring—but our first priority is to have a healthy pet that serves his real purpose of being a friend and companion.

Reputable breeders think of the standard as a pattern of perfection and strive to produce animals that fit it. Studying the standard is a prerequisite for purchasing a Bulldog. You should know something about the special dog you are going to buy. Is a Bulldog what you really want? Use your head as well as your heart. Buying a dog, any dog, is a commitment of ten to fifteen years and is not to be taken lightly.

The Bulldog Standard

A copy of the Bulldog standard can be obtained from the American Kennel Club, 51 Madison Ave., New York, NY 10010, (212) 696-8200, or you can go to the local library and look in the non-sporting section of *The Complete Dog Book*.

To help you understand the Bulldog, this chapter will discuss some of the unique and important features of the Bulldog as stated in the standard. Direct quotes from the standard are given in italics, and the author's comments follow.

General Appearance

The perfect Bulldog must be medium in size and smooth coat, with heavy, thick set, low swung body, massive short-faced head, wide shoulders, sturdy limbs. The general appearance and attitude should suggest great stability, vigor and strength.

Medium size is about 50 pounds for mature males and 40 pounds for mature females. This is not true today: Most males will be in the 55 to 65 pound category and females in the 45 to 50 pound range.

The disposition should be equable and kind, resolute and courageous (not vicious or aggressive) and demeanor should be pacific and dignified. This attitude should be countenanced by expression and behavior.

By stating this in the first paragraphs of the standard, the authors stressed that disposition and attitude are as important as conformation or appearance. The Bulldog is a decorous, self-respecting, confident animal. She does not pick fights, but once attacked will defend herself and protect the people she cares about.

In the absence of her master, the Bulldog might invite an intruder in, show him about and then lead him to the silverware. Because the Bulldog's general appearance belies her demeanor, the intruder may not accept the invitation and the silverware may remain intact and safe.

In the beginning, Bulldogs were bred for bull-baiting and fighting. If the dog was to survive, she had to be lean, agile and athletic. With the outlawing of this inhumane, vicious sport, the purpose of the dog changed and so did her appearance. She became a companion, a gentle loving friend, and somewhat of a couch potato.

SYMMETRY

Many breeders and judges refer to the Bulldog as a "head" breed, as the head is definitely its trademark. For judging purposes, numerical points are assigned to various parts of the dog. Although the Bulldog is a head breed, the total number of points allotted to various parts of the head is exactly the same as the number of points possible for the body—thirty-nine each.

These equal points assignments are supported by the following statement from the standard on symmetry:

The "points" should be well distributed and bear good relation one to the other, no feature being in such prominence from either excess or lack of quality that the animal appears deformed or ill proportioned.

GAIT

The style and carriage are peculiar, his gait being a loose-jointed shuffling, side wise motion giving the characteristic "roll." The action must, however, be unrestrained, free and vigorous.

The Bulldog should have a free and vigorous gait.

This peculiar gait is the result of the heavy, wide shoulders, short front legs with longer hind legs and narrow rear. In spite of all this, the Bulldog can move quickly and jump a reasonable height (such as upon your bed, or into the back of the van when it is show time).

COAT AND COLOR

The coat is short, smooth and fine. The preferred colors are (1) Red Brindle (2) all other Brindles (3) solid white (4) solid red, fawn (5) pie bald (6) inferior qualities of all the foregoing. Only solid black is objectionable.

The standard states clearly the preferred colors, but like beauty, the preferred color is really in the eyes of the beholder. However, if everything else is correct about the dog you want, learn to like his color!

SKIN

The skin should be soft and loose, especially at the head, neck and shoulders.

It almost seems like the Bulldog has more skin than he needs. His head and face are covered with wrinkles that form a pattern which helped the Bulldog when bullfighting—they kept the bull's blood away from the dog's eyes and nose during the actual attack.

THE HEAD

Skull

The skull should be very large, and in circumference, in front of the ears, should measure at least the height of the dog at the shoulders.

Note the "at least." The dogs of today have shorter legs than those of 100 years ago. Today the Bulldog's skull will measure more than $1\frac{1}{4}$ times the height at the dog's shoulders, or it will be considered too small.

Cheeks

The cheeks should be well-rounded, protruding sideways and outward beyond the eyes.

Stop

The temples or frontal bones should be very well defined, broad, square and high, causing a hollow or groove between the eyes. This indentation, or stop, should be both broad and deep and extend up the middle of the forehead, dividing the head vertically, being traceable to the top of the skull.

Eyes and Eyelids

The eyes seen from the front should be situated low down in the skull, as far from the ears as possible and their corners should be in a straight line at right angle with the stop.

This simply says his eyes should be placed at the point where the forehead and cheeks meet. They are round in shape and very dark. If the eyes of man are windows to his soul, the eyes of the Bulldog are certainly windows to his personality—they portray kindness, gentleness and interest. They are alert but not looking for trouble.

Ears

The ears should be set high in the head, the front inner edge of each joining the outline of the skull, so as to place them as wide apart, and as high and as far from the eyes as possible. In size they are small and thin. The shape termed "rose ear" is the most desirable. The "rose ear" folds inward at its back lower edge curving over, outwards and backwards, showing part of the inside of the burr.

Your Bulldog's ears can tell you a lot about her mood.

The Bulldog's expression depends greatly upon the proper shape and carriage of the ears. Prick ears (upright), tulip ears (bent over at the tip), or ears that lie flat to her skull are highly objectionable.

Face

The face is extremely short—muzzle very short, broad, turned upward. The nose is large, broad, black and the tip is set deeply between his eyes. Because of this placement of the nose, the dog can breathe as he hangs on to the bull and the "wrinkle pattern" prevents the blood from the bull getting into his nose.

Bite and Jaws

The jaws should be very massive, very broad, square and "undershot," the lower jaw projecting considerably in front of the upper jaw and turning up.

This undershot bite makes it possible for the dog to hang on almost indefinitely.

NECK

The neck should be very short, very thick, deep and strong and well arched at the back.

The proper topline begins with the neck, which must be long enough that his head doesn't appear to be sitting on his shoulders.

THE BODY
Shoulders
The shoulders should be muscular, very heavy, wide spread and slanting outward, giving stability and great power.

The Bulldog's chest is very broad and the front legs are short, straight, muscular and set wide apart. The calves of the legs are very well-developed. Because of this, the dog appears "bow-legged." Not so! The bones are straight and the appearance is only an optical illusion.

Brisket and Body
The brisket and body should be very capacious with full sides, well rounded ribs and very deep from the shoulders down to its lowest part where it joins the chest. It should be well let down between the shoulders and forelegs giving the dog a broad, low, short-legged appearance. The body should be well ribbed up behind with the belly tucked up and not rotund.

Champion or not, your Bulldog will be a loving part of your family.

The brisket as defined by Dr. Edward Vardons is the forepart of the body below the chest, between the forelegs, closest to the ribs.

The standard is saying that if the dog walked upright on his hind legs, he would be a caricature of a wrestler: heavy, muscular arms, large chest and rib cage and small waist.

Back and Topline
There should be a slight fall in the back, close behind the shoulders (the lowest part) whence the spine should rise to the

13

loins (the top of which should be higher than that of the shoulders (hind legs are longer than the front legs) thence curving again more suddenly to the tail, forming an arch (a very distinctive feature of the breed) termed "roached" back or more correctly "wheel" back, this forms the top line that is unique to the bulldog.

The back should be short and strong, very broad at the shoulders and comparatively narrow at the loins.

Hind Legs

The hind legs should be strong and muscular and longer than the forelegs, so as to elevate the loins above the shoulders.

Feet

The feet are moderate in size, compact and firmly set. Toes compact, well split up, with high knuckles and short stubby nails.

The front feet may be straight or turned slightly outward, but the hind feet should be pointed well outward.

Your Bulldog may have either a straight or screwed tail.

Tail

The tail may be either straight or "screwed" but never curved or curly and in any case must be short, hung low and with a decided downward carriage, thick root and fine tip. If the tail is straight, it should be cylindrical and uniform taper. If "screwed" the bends or kinks should be well defined, and they *may be abrupt and even knotty, but no portion of the member should be elevated above the base or root.*

The tail is never docked. It may appear too long at birth, but puppies grow faster than their tails. If the puppy is born without a tail, this is a serious fault and may indicate future problems.

What's Not to Love?

A pet Bulldog will not have everything as the standard states (I've never seen a dog who does), but with the Bulldog personality, he will be a wonderful, loving member of your family. Be concerned, but not too concerned, about his looks. Few of us could walk the runway of a beauty pageant, but our lives have been successful, and so it is with the ordinary Bulldog! His devotion is just as great as (maybe greater than) that of his champion relatives.

The Bulldog's History

How the Bulldog Got Its Name

Authorities differ so completely about the origin of the Bulldog that the name itself is in dispute. While some feel that the breed may derive its name from the bulllike shape of its head, others maintain that the name came from the ancient custom of using Bulldogs in the sport of bullbaiting.

There appears to be little doubt, however, that an early canine species resembling the Bulldog has been in existence for centuries.

Some early references indicate that the oldest English spelling of the name was probably "Bondogge" or "Bolddogge." Later, the name "Banddogge" was mentioned by the English playwright William

Shakespeare (1564–1616) in act 1, scene VI of the play *King Henry VI*: "The time when screech owls cry and Banddogges howl and spirits walk and ghosts break up their graves."

Possibly the first use of the modern spelling is found in a letter dated in 1631, written to George Willingham of St. Swithins Lane, London, from Prestwick Eaton of St. Sabestion, requesting "two good mastiffs and two good bulldogs." That letter seems to establish that Bulldogs and Mastiffs were two distinct breeds of dogs in England.

Origins of the Breed

Both the Bulldog and the Mastiff are believed to have a common origin in the extinct breed known as the "alaunt," also spelled "alaune" or "allan." The allan of Geoffrey Chaucer's time (1340–1400) was a dog described as having great strength and courage, and used for chasing the lion and the bear.

Cotsgraves English-French dictionary, published in 1632, describes the Allan de Bouchere, which was used to bring in the oxen, as being similar in appearance to the modern Mastiff.

In the description of the alaunts, or allans, there are three distinct Bulldog characteristics which remain to this day. The alaunts were said to have large, thick heads and short muzzles. They were extremely courageous, and when attacked, they hung on to their opponent by their teeth.

Banddogges or Bulldogs also were known to have been crossbred with various other breeds for the purpose of correcting the other breeds' lack of courage, tenacity and determination.

Early Bulldogs were heavier than they are today, although they have always maintained an exceptional degree of tenacity and stamina. The early Bulldogs were also quite powerful, ferocious animals. In temperament, however, they were not the soft-hearted, friendly companions of the modern era.

17

BULL-BAITING

There can be no doubt that the Bulldog was originally bred for the purpose of bull- and bear-baiting, as well as for fighting other dogs.

At that time, the Bulldog was quite large, weighing from 80 to 100 pounds or more. The sport of bull-baiting was popular with all classes of English society, particularly around London and the Midlands. There were bullrings and dog pits in many areas.

In the beginning the dog would attack the bull by the ear and hang on until the bull was exhausted or his

Champion Don-allen Lord Stuart, owned by Ken and Tracey James.

ear was torn off. Later, the bull's nose was the target and a smaller, quicker dog was more efficient. The dogs were also used to attack bulls and cows that were to be slaughtered. People believed that the meat from these bruised animals was more tender.

Dogfighting was very popular with the lower classes of English society. The dogs used in this sport were trained to be vicious animals; they were so dangerous that they had to be tied or confined at all times. Otherwise, they would try to fight and kill everything in sight. There are stories about the Bulldog's ability to tolerate and ignore pain, and of Bulldogs whose legs were amputated during fights but continued to attack. There are even pictures of dogs with their bellies ripped open, hanging on to the bull's nose and flying through the air. This kind of cruelty is best forgotten, but we honor and remember those men and women who outlawed this horrible sport.

The Evolving Bulldog

Selective breeding brought into being the Bulldog of today, who is as loving and loyal as his predecessors were vicious and mean. The inhumane practice of bull-baiting was finally outlawed in Great Britain in 1835. The breeding of Bulldogs soon diminished, since they apparently no longer served a useful purpose.

The banning of bull-baiting almost resulted in the extinction of the Bulldog. Had it not been for a handful of Englishmen who saw the virtue of preserving this exceptional breed, the breeding of Bulldogs might have ceased altogether. Among these men was William George, who devoted himself to securing a more honorable status for the breed. Breaking away from the low and cruel practice of dogfighting, he named his kennel "Kensel Rise," or "Canine Castle." There he produced several outstanding dogs, one of which was Young King Dick, who was reputed to be a remarkable specimen of that era.

After bull-baiting was made illegal, Bulldogs were bred to be loyal and loving.

Recent research reveals that the first known written description of the breed was produced in 1860 on a parchment scroll in England. The first class for Bulldogs at a dog show was at Birmingham, England, also in 1860.

BULLDOG CLUBS

The first Bulldog club, simply named The Bulldog Club, with the motto "Hold Fast," was organized in

England on November 3, 1864, by thirty members whose stated objective was "the perpetuation and the improvement of the old English bulldog."

The Bulldog Club's major accomplishment during its three-year existence was the drafting in 1865 of the first Bulldog standard ever published. It was written by the club's treasurer, Samuel Wickens, and was referred to as the Philo-Kuon standard—which was actually the author's *nom de plume*, or pen name.

For the next ten years, the number of Bulldogs entered at shows began to increase, and classes for dogs and bitches were offered in various weight categories from 12 pounds to 25 pounds and over. However, it was not long until some Spanish Bulldogs, who weighed as much as 100 pounds, began to be imported—a situation the English breeders believed could again threaten the existence of the purebred English Bulldog.

In March 1875, a group of English breeders met and reconstituted the former Bulldog Club at a London public house called the Blue Post. (The pub still exists today at Newman and Oxford Streets, but has been renamed the Rose and Crown.)

At this time a written standard of perfection for the breed, describing the complete anatomy of the Bulldog, was formulated and published on May 27, 1875. A table of points for the standard was adopted by the club and published on September 2, 1875.

Bulldogs in the USA

The first Bulldog to be exhibited in America, a dog named Donald, who was whelped in 1875, was shown at New York in 1880 by Sir William Verner. Donald, who was brindle and white, reportedly weighed about 40 pounds and was sired by Alpha ex Vixen.

The first Bulldog registered in the United States and recorded as Number 4982 in the AKC Stud Book was a brindle and white dog named Bob, sired by Taurus ex Millie and owned by Thomas Patten of Appleton,

Wisconsin. In 1888, the first English-bred Bulldog, a dog named Robinson Crusoe, achieved American Kennel Club championship status.

In 1896, the first American-bred Bulldog was recognized by the AKC as a champion; he was Ch Rodney L Ambassadeur, a male owned and bred by Charles Hopton. Hopton was a successful breeder on both sides of the Atlantic, and his Rodney kennel prefix was said to denote both quality and soundness in the breed. The first American-bred Bulldog bitch to attain her AKC championship was Ch Princess Merlow, owned by Harry Ruston.

Developing an American Standard

Americans used the English conformation standard until a committee was formed in 1894 to modify it. The club officially adopted what was believed to be a more informative, concisely worded standard in 1896.

Revised only twice since its adoption in 1896, the American conformation standard remains almost entirely intact. Its first revision on September 5, 1914, deleted the highly undesirable "butterfly or parti-colored" nose and inserted the words "Dudley or flesh-colored" as the breed's only disqualifying fault. The latest revision, approved by the AKC on July 20, 1976, deleted the terms "Dudley or flesh-colored nose" and substituted the terms "Brown or liver colored nose" as the disqualifying fault.

Bulldog Club of America (BCA)

English Bulldogs were being imported, bred and shown in the United States about ten years before H.D. Kendall, a breeder from Lowell, Massachusetts, conceived the idea of forming a Bulldog club in the United States.

The purpose of the organization was "to join together for the purpose of encouraging the thoughtful and careful breeding of the English Bulldog in America, to perpetuate the purity of the strain, to improve the quality of native stock and to remove the undesirable prejudice that existed in the public mind against a most admirable breed."

Thus, the Bulldog Club of America was formed by a group of eight interested fanciers at a New England Kennel Club all-breed dog show in Boston on April 1, 1890. The club was incorporated in New York state on February 29, 1904. Often referred to as the breed's parent club, the Bulldog Club of America, Inc. is one of the oldest active purebred dog clubs in the United States.

Since the club's purposes and objectives can be found in the forward of the organization's constitution, it is not necessary to state them here in their entirety. Briefly stated, they encourage members to (1) maintain a current conformation standard, (2) improve the quality of the breed, (3) compete in dog shows, (4) publicly promote the Bulldog and (5) work together for the general good of all Bulldog breeders, owners and exhibitors.

At the end of the first fiscal year in March 1891, the BCA had attracted a total of thirty members. By 1904, as the breed became more popular, membership in the club grew to seventy-six, and in 1909 there were 132 active members.

Most of the club activities and members were from the East Coast and membership growth was very slow. About fifty years later there were 267 members.

Following World War II, there was a successful movement to revise the club's original constitution and bylaws and to broaden the club's appeal. The reorganization that followed decentralized the club's structure and expanded the club's activities across the nation.

The BCA Today
The BCA's current constitution and bylaws were adopted by the membership on January 13, 1950, and approved by the AKC on February 10, 1950.

Under the new constitution and bylaws, the club divided into eight divisions or geographic regions, each with its own officers and board of directors. The national organization was retained, but its four national officers are elected every two years from within one of the eight BCA Divisions on a rotating basis.

After the reorganization membership increased at a steady pace and at this time there are over 3,000 members and fifty-eight local clubs in the eight divisions.

The purpose of these clubs is to have annual dog shows. But more importantly, these clubs strive to protect the Bulldog from unethical breeders, and to have ongoing educational programs and seminars. The integrity of the breed is, of course, of great importance to the clubs.

If you want to continue to learn about Bulldogs, membership in the BCA is a wise investment.

The Bulldogger

In 1972 *The Bulldogger* (the official publication of BCA) was launched. It is distributed without charge to all BCA members and judges.

The Bulldogger contains articles on many and varied subjects by members and veterinarians, as well as owners and breeders of other breeds of dogs. There are show reports, information on upcoming shows and pictures of dogs. There is a section with questions and answers, in which questions are answered by breeders and owners according to their experiences.

The breeder of your puppy should be able to give you the name and address of a local BCA affiliate, but if that is not an option, the American Kennel Club can direct you to the national offices (AKC's address is in chapter 1).

The Symbolic Bulldog

The breeders and fanciers of the Bulldog have taken part in a remarkable process of evolution. Although it has taken many, many years, a snarling, fighting, aggressive animal has been changed into a gentle, quiet animal. Bulldogs have gone from bull-baiting arenas and fighting rings to becoming the beloved mascots of football teams. Many colleges have the Bulldog as their sports mascot because of the Bulldog's history of giving his all to be the winner. Today we expect to see the Yale Bulldog or the Butler Bulldog sitting at the bench of his respective team. Many high schools throughout the nation also have Bulldog mascots, hoping that the Bulldog tenacity will somehow rub off on their team.

Advertisers are using the Bulldog more and more to attract public attention to their products. The term "Bulldog grip" is often used to describe the hold of various tools, especially wrenches and pliers. The Bulldog's appearance is unique and he gives a good account of himself before the camera.

The Bulldog who played "Lucky Dog" entertained us at dog shows as he toted his Purina dog food. Many of us enjoyed the television series "Jake and the Fatman" because we always anxiously awaited the appearance of Max (Champion Breckley Buford Win and Grin). In addition to his skills as an entertainer, this dog won his conformation championship and CD title all in one year. He brought honor to the breed and joy to his owners.

Obedience Competition and Beyond

A few years ago it was rare to see Bulldogs in obedience competition because the general opinion was that they were too dumb, too stubborn and too clumsy to learn or jump. Not true! What is true is that the Bulldog is "his own man." He is not a robot or windup toy. The Bulldog is intelligent and can jump according to his bodily conformation.

Bulldoggers decided to prove to the public that the Bulldog can hold his own in obedience competition and today they are doing just that! Bulldogs are also being taught tracking and carting. Some are quite adept in agility tests. Bulldogs today are everywhere!

Bulldogs hold their own in obedience competitions.

CROWD PLEASERS

Bulldogs can go through obedience paces quickly and precisely with little error. Like their human friends, Bulldogs respond to audience approval and applause. On some days, your Bulldog will follow commands with a lot of accuracy. On other days, "sitting," "staying" or "jumping hurdles" is just not on the program. She may seem to be thinking, "Why today? I did this yesterday and maybe I will again tomorrow, but not today!" Bulldogs have minds of their own.

A few Bulldog breeders believed that given half a chance, the Bulldog could and would make a great effort in the obedience ring. At all breed shows, when a Bulldog was entered in obedience, he attracted a great deal of attention. Some days he was a clown—other days he would perform like a dignified gentleman.

FAMOUS OWNERS OF BULLDOGS

Colette

Ice-T

Calvin Coolidge

Frances Day

Olivia de Havilland

Stan Lee

Nancy Mitford

Vincent Price

Tennessee Williams

Woodrow Wilson

A demonstration of Bulldogs and their ability in obedience was first introduced at the annual BCA National Week in 1988 by Anne Hier (now a part of the AKC staff). This created enough interest that the Council voted to have obedience competition at the next BCA National to be held in Houston, Texas, in 1989. More and more Bulldogs began appearing in obedience in the all-breed shows—doing quite well. They continued to be Bulldogs, keeping their handlers alert, and their audiences awed at times and profoundly amused at others.

The Bulldog's tenacious personality lends to her talent in carting.

BULLDOGS ON THE MARCH

California breeders and fanciers have proven that Bulldogs have many hidden talents. At the National BCA show in 1996, we were astounded to see a Drill Team of Bulldogs marching right, left, forward—the same commands that drill teams are given, as precise and sharp as West Point Cadets. We watched a little female Bulldog go through the agility routine—bounding, jumping and having fun. There were thirty-five entries in obedience and an even greater audience observing as the dogs went through their paces. The Californian bulldoggers believe the dogs can perform in tracking, and their Bulldogs do. True, with their short noses they almost stand on their heads when locating the "scent" and track, but they are successful nonetheless. They should be commended for showing the world that the "ugly" Bulldog is not only beautiful, but is useful too. There are bulldoggers throughout the United States doing obedience, etc., but the majority are in California.

After training, Bulldogs perform admirably as therapy dogs. It is difficult to tell who is the happiest—the patient who needs to be loved or the dog who is giving love.

How Popularity Harms

Bulldog breeders and owners have a sincere interest in protecting the breed from attempted over-breeding. To some extent the Bulldog herself provides some protection. Bulldogs are not prolific breeders—their litters are small (as compared to many other breeds of dogs) and cesarean sections are almost always necessary, so the initial cost of breeding is greater than with most other breeds.

Bulldog breeders recognize that there are too many puppies being born (of all breeds) each year that will become homeless and die horrible, untimely deaths. Homeless dogs are known to destroy property and be a general nuisance. Breeders do not want this fate for Bulldogs (or any dog) so, under the direction of BCA, a "Bulldog Rescue" was established. Humane societies know who to call in their area if a Bulldog is brought to them; veterinarians also know who to call if they receive an unwanted Bulldog. At the expense of BCA, this homeless, unwanted animal is given a complete physical examination, treated and neutered and will soon be ready for a new home that has been evaluated for suitability. For a reasonable sum, the new owner has a dog. The dog is to be returned to "Rescue" if for some reason she can no longer stay in the new home. Many other breed

Rescued Bulldogs make loving pets and can be adopted with a minimal fee.

organizations have established the same type of "Rescue" program.

Breeding dogs and owning dogs are commitments—not just whims to be enjoyed for a couple of days and then forgotten. It has been said that the measure of a man can be taken by the way he treats children and dogs!

The **World**
According to the
Bulldog

Today's Bulldogs make wonderful pets in spite of the fighting temperament they were encouraged to possess generations ago. According to the AKC, they were "bred from a long line of fighting ancestors, they grew to be so savage, so courageous as to be almost insensitive to pain." After many years of careful breeding, however, all of the Bulldog's excellent

qualities have been retained. Within a few generations, the Bulldog became "one of the finest physical specimens, minus its original viciousness."

You have read carefully what the hierarchy of Bulldog experts says a Bulldog should look like and a little about what he is. However, there is nothing like getting to know the wonderful personalities of individual Bulldogs to tell you what this breed is really like. It is certainly a breed of distinct individuals. Some of my dogs have been excellent show specimens whose influences can be seen in some of the dogs in the ring today; some never darkened the door of a show. All these Bulldogs, show greats or homebodies, were wonderful because of the great spirits housed in their small bodies. Your Bulldog will have his own unique and wonderful personality, and will leave you and your family with many wonderful Bulldog memories of your own.

Bulldogs Are People Dogs

If you already own a Bulldog, you know that people are her thing. Given a little training she is a wonderful therapy dog. Her kindness and gentleness when approaching the aged and infirm are a joy to behold.

One Bulldog called Kelley Boy was always ready to go to the nursing home to brighten the patients' day. One such patient had refused to talk to the attendants or other patients, but Kelley Boy's presence must have touched some past memory, as she had tears in her eyes when she stroked his head and said "Good dog!" This helped her begin to finally communicate. Kelley Boy was a conformation champion but his real contribution was the happiness he brought to this woman.

CHARACTERISTICS OF THE BULLDOG
Tenacious
Loyal
Loving
Good with kids
Dislikes rain
Likes routine
Thrives on attention

I attended the wake of a friend, a very old lady who had the companionship of a Bulldog for the last years of her life. Her family, realizing that the dog's grief was as real and deep as their own, allowed the dog to be in the room where the deceased was lying.

When no person was at the casket paying their last respects, the dog was lying by the casket. As each person would go up to the casket, the dog would get up and stand, and in her own way seemed to say "thank you for coming." This dog lived only a few weeks after her friend of years died.

Goldie to the Rescue

Bulldogs are adaptable to almost any person who really wants one, but some people are not compatible with them. Some Bulldogs are content in a boisterous, happy and busy family. Others would be miserable in a home with constant commotion. Goldie was a beautiful young female. Her appearance gave the promise of a great show career, but she was retiring and quiet. Riding in a car terrified her and she hated dog shows, but she loved the old gentleman who lived next door. He was feeble and unsteady as he walked about on his lawn. It was at these times that Goldie would go up to him, slowly and quietly waiting for a pat on the head and a kind word.

One morning Goldie dashed out the door, across the lawn and up the steps of her friend's house. She was barking frantically, and Goldie never barked! She refused to come home. Her bark was becoming louder and more urgent. So, with leash in hand and anger in my walk, I went after my noisy, disobedient dog. As I reached down to put the leash on Goldie, I heard a faint, weak cry for help. I pushed the door open—on the floor lay the old gentleman with the telephone just out of his reach. Because Goldie heard and recognized this distress signal, help came and her friend lived several more years.

Kids and Bulldogs

The Bulldog seems to understand that babies and little children are special and need special treatment. He will tolerate their poking and prodding, but if a child gets too rough, the dog will simply leave. However, in all fairness to the dog and for the safety of children, until the children understand the proper approach to an animal, they should not be left alone together. Small children and puppies are not a good combination.

Some people believe a puppy and a baby must grow up together if the puppy is to accept the child. This is not necessarily true. Some toddlers think puppies are toys. They like to poke at the puppy's eyes or pull at his ears or maybe use the puppy to sit upon. The puppy might think the toddler is something to chew. When the pup tries to defend himself by biting, he is reprimanded, although he has really only protected himself from the curious toddler.

Neither the puppy nor the toddler is mature. Wait to get a puppy until the toddler becomes a child and can understand that puppies are not toys and can be injured. If you do get a puppy, get one that is at lease 6 months of age for a child under 3 years of age. A baby in diapers and a puppy not housebroken are too much! A 6-month-old puppy should be easily house-broken and hopefully a 3-year-old child will be toilet trained.

All interaction between puppies and children should be closely supervised.

One of my most wonderful Bulldog characters was Molly Morovalaunt, or Mugsy. She was an AKC regis-tered English Bulldog. Mugsy protected my children; I could not even discipline them if she was present.

Mugsy couldn't stand to hear a child cry! The sound of a child crying called for an investigation on her part that included a washing of the face and hands of the little one in distress.

In training, Mugsy learned to leap for and take a gun from her tormentor even if the gun was being fired. She learned to attack on command anyone who might try to do harm to me or my boys. This was all learned for the sake of watching over the family should the need arise.

Bulldogs Like Routine

If you take your Bulldog for a daily morning walk, he will come to expect it and may even bring his leash to you. (Unless it's raining—most Bulldogs do not like to walk in the rain, or through puddles after a rain.) Dogs tend to get up at about the same time each day, and go to bed at about the same time each night.

BUTCH

Sometimes Bulldogs will establish their own routines. One day a Bulldog named Butch and his owner appeared at the door of our clinic. Butch had a terrible infestation of fleas and ticks. After he was treated, home he went—fleas gone, itching gone. Unfortunately, science had not yet developed a pill that controls fleas.

About three weeks later Butch was back, covered with fleas and standing at our gate waiting to get in. He would not leave until he was treated. This procedure was repeated about every three weeks. Butch and his fleas would show up, and Butch would leave once again without the fleas. If you were the veterinarian, to whom would you send a bill? Or would you send a bill?

INTRODUCING NEW THINGS

Sometimes a Bulldog's need for routine can turn up in unusual and unexpected ways, as in the case of Iggy. Iggy was a wonderful mother; she was a peacemaker and she loved her home just as it was, with its familiar old, comfortable chairs and davenports. I never understood why these things meant anything to her because none of the dogs were allowed on the furniture—except my bed when I was in it.

One day while browsing around a furniture store, a leather chair caught my eye—it seemed to be saying "take me home," but my purse would not allow it. The chair won out and was delivered a few days later as a replacement for an old, threadbare chair.

Iggy immediately noticed what she saw as an impostor chair, but seemed to accept the change. I had never had any real damage done to anything in the house by my dogs. The sad ending is that Iggy destroyed this chair beyond repair.

I should have introduced the chair more slowly—and this is the way a new dog or puppy should be introduced into the household. Allow a new dog and old dog to do their "doggy" introductory sniffing. (I am assuming that the dogs are the same sex or have been neutered if both are mature dogs. It is too much to ask any mature animal to ignore the hormonal call.) After a short time, crate the new dog and spend time with the permanent resident, assuring her that she is number one and very much loved. Maybe give her a special treat or a new bone to chew. *Repeat this* several times daily until the dogs are comfortable with each other. However, don't leave them alone—like children, one child can play alone without creating havoc. Two children may make the playroom a complete disaster. In time, they will become fast friends and, like my Bethie and Cleo, get their bones at about 3 o'clock each afternoon and lie in the middle of the floor chewing and exchanging gossip.

> **LADDIE**
>
> I was 9 years old when my father (a farmer) brought my first Bulldog home in his overcoat pocket. He paid $5.00 for the pup and my mother was angry! Five dollars was a lot of money and was needed for the basic necessities of life. Since I had no siblings at the time and lived in a rural area without close neighbors, Laddie was my playmate. When I was older and boys came to call, some would leave very abruptly if Laddie appeared—much to the amusement and delight of my father. Laddie didn't look much like a Bulldog—but his personality was all Bulldog!

Sleeping Habits

Bulldogs are usually delighted to share your bed or sleep on their own in your bedroom. Beware, most Bulldogs snore! They do not have a quiet, soft snore. It is a loud, regular snore. To the seasoned Bulldog owner this snore is music—an indication that all is right in the household. To others, it is a raucous annoyance. If you are someone who must have absolute silence in your bedroom, then the Bulldog must sleep at the other side of the house.

If for some reason it is impossible for him to share your bedroom, then a permanent spot should be selected. A laundry or utility room, if it is cool in the summer, warm in the winter, is ideal. A wire crate with a blanket or rug (not indoor-outdoor carpeting) for a bed is the next best thing to sharing your bed. This setup also gives the Bulldog a place of his own during the day. He can go there as he wishes, or you can put him there and close the door should you have guests who cannot tolerate or do not appreciate dogs.

The very worst thing that can happen to a Bulldog is to be ignored. Once he knows your routine, he wants to share, and may do any number of things to be the recipient of your attention and affection. Mugsy, for example, was a show-off and a ham. She was happiest when doing her repertoire of tricks—putting out matches, refusing a piece of delectable meat that she was told was poison and many others. She knew what sit and stay meant and obeyed so diligently that one time I forgot that I had commanded her to sit and stay in a local lumberyard office, until four

A crate is a place your Bulldog can call his very own.

hours later I was called to come and get her. She had never moved from the position I left her in.

Unpleasant Noises?

Some Bulldogs are prone to flatulence, which is generally due to improper diet. A change of food will be an essential factor in controlling this unpleasant occurrence.

Bulldogs Need Exercise

Although the Bulldog doesn't exactly crave exercise, it is important that she get it. Exercise is necessary for maintaining her good health, just as it is for keeping her human friends in their prime. A walk at a brisk pace will be good for both you and your dog. Having your Bulldog chase and retrieve a ball gets her running about as well.

Exercise is an essential part of keeping your Bulldog healthy.

HEALTH PRECAUTIONS

Bulldogs are bracycephalic (short muzzled) and they tend to overheat easily. Dogs do not perspire over their entire body and are only cooled by panting and through the pads of their feet, so extra precaution must be taken during hot weather. Walk in the early morning or after sundown. *Never* leave your dog in the car, even if the windows are down. Stationary cars become very hot in just a few minutes and are virtual death traps.

Bulldogs Like Other Pets

Bulldogs not only like people—they like other dogs and cats (if they grow up together). They will clean each other's wrinkles and ears. Every afternoon at 3 o'clock, Bethie (12 years old) and Cleo lie in the middle of the living room chewing their respective bones. This is a regular ritual and if necessary I could set the clock by their afternoon bone chewing. This kind of friendship would be difficult between a male and female, unless the male was neutered and the female spayed.

Some Bulldogs may not get along that well with other animals. Mugsy, for example, hated cats with an overwhelming passion, and any cat coming in sight of her puppies quickly found itself in the face of danger. This hatred of cats was an extension of an overactive maternal instinct. When she had puppies she growled at everyone except me when they came near her pups. She never bit anyone, but they respected the growl and did not trespass. After the puppies left her nest, cats were not in danger of losing one of their nine lives—but never were they welcome guests.

Mugsy loved all puppies—but confusion and concern showed in her face when her own puppies died and we gave her a Dachshund pup. Oh yes, she washed, fed, and disciplined the long, lean, skinny-tailed baby, but she seemed to be trying to figure out what went wrong.

One day Mugsy and I found ourselves foster parents to a tiny premature lamb called Mary. As I would prepare and feed the formula, Mugsy would wash Mary's face and let her cuddle up. Soon the lamb was as big as her foster mother and too mischievous to be kept indoors.

Your Bulldog doesn't have to be a show champion to be the champion of your heart.

Despite the change, Mugsy and Mary did not lose their bond. Whenever Mary could, she would play with and tease Mugsy. Mary accepted Mugsy for the Bulldog she was and Mugsy accepted Mary with her long legs and woolly coat. Somewhere in this acceptance is a lesson to be learned.

Bulldogs Love Life

Mike was one of Mugsy's sons. Mike's owner, who owned and operated a large car dealership, was an important man in the town. The dog was so beloved that on the side of the car garage, bigger than life, was a painted picture of Mike riding as engineer in a recreational train.

Mike was not only known to the people of the town, but also to the merchants—especially to the local retail store manager and the meat market owner next door.

Several times a week, Mike would leave home (several blocks from his planned destination) and go across streets and a state highway to the large retail store. There he sat patiently at the entrance until the opportunity came to slip quickly in and up the stairs to the ladies department. The lady customers squealed, the manager bounded up the stairs and down went Mike out the door!

There he would sit for a few minutes, catch his breath while pondering the situation and then quietly and deliberately go to the back door of the meat market to wait and wait. Finally the butcher appeared with part of a cow's leg to give to Mike. Then home he went at last to enjoy his bone and snooze in the sun.

Not everyone approved of Mike and his trekking about town (including me), but we all remember him. This Bulldog enjoyed life, and thought everyone loved him as much as he loved them.

The Traveling Bulldog

Bulldogs are good travelers in the car and excellent guests in a motel. The best and safest way for your Bulldog to travel is in a crate that fits in the back of your car and can be anchored safely onto the actual seat. If your dog is in the back of a van, he will probably lie down and sleep. If the crate is anchored onto the back seat he may be able to look out and watch the world go by.

TRAVEL SUPPLIES

Just as you pack things you will need when you travel, your dog will need things too. Remember to take a roll of paper towels, rugs or blankets for the floor of the crate, her regular food, a small pooper-scooper and quart-size baggies, a gallon jug of water, water and food dishes, an extra leash and an old shower curtain or 6'×6' piece of plastic to put under the crate in the motel room. Don't forget any medication your Bulldog may be taking.

There are water dishes that clip on the inside of the crates that make it easy for your dog to drink while traveling. If you travel frequently, a good investment is a second wire crate to take into the motel. The car crate is anchored and the second crate eliminates the need to re-anchor the car crate daily. Also, the dog remains safe in the crate while the second crate is being taken into the motel and set up for her. These wire crates fold and take up very little room.

The 6'×6' plastic underneath the crate wire keeps bits of food and hair off the carpet. We who travel with our dogs must make every effort to respect the rights of others and be good guests. Being respectful means cleaning up after your dog, keeping her in the crate while you are out of the room and keeping her quiet. Hopefully, the walls are thick so her snores are not heard by the next-door neighbor.

If you must travel by air, be sure she is on a nonstop flight and is in an approved airline crate. Do not put her into the crate until the very last minute and watch until she is put on the plane. Do not travel in hot or sub-zero weather. Bulldogs are really not good air travelers.

Dog Sitters and Kennels

If you must leave him at home, the least traumatic situation is to keep your dog in his familiar surroundings and have someone he knows come about four times daily, allow him to exercise, have some playtime and be fed. This is satisfactory for two or three days, but for any longer length of time a boarding kennel is best. The kennel should be heated in the winter and air conditioned in the summer (especially if the dog is in air conditioning at home). Most kennels will appreciate it if you bring the food he is accustomed to along with a favorite toy and bed.

Leave the name and telephone number of your veterinarian and instruct the attendants to call him if the need arises. Your veterinarian should be told that he may be called if something comes up. A health certificate is required when traveling by air and some boarding kennels also require them, so immunizations must be current.

A final note: If you have in-home care, be sure the person you are leaving your dog with is trustworthy and really cares about your Bulldog. He, too, should be authorized to call the veterinarian as necessary.

Boarding kennels should be visited before you leave your dog. Note cleanliness, how the boarded dogs look and if there are twenty-four hour attendants. Be comfortable with the people with whom and the surroundings in which you will be leaving your dog.

More Information on Bulldogs

BOOKS

Berndt, Dr. Robert. *Your Bulldog.* Virginia: Denlingers Pub Ltd., 1975.

Hanes, Col. Bailey C. *The New Bulldog.* New York: Howell Book House, 1991.

McGibbon, John F. *The Bulldog Yesterday, Today &* *Tomorrow.* New York: Howell Book House, 1996.

NATIONAL BREED CLUB

National Bulldog Club
Susan Rodenski
480 Bully Hill Dr.
King George, VI 22485
(540) 775-3015

This club can send you information on all aspects of the breed, including the names and addresses of breed clubs in your area, as well as obedience clubs. Inquire about membership.

Other Bulldog Clubs

American Bulldog Association
HC 67, Box 117
Bruno, AZ 72618
(510) 449-4644
online: *bulldog@mtnhome.com*

Bulldog Club of America
Robert Church, President
3604 Prestwick Dr.
Tucker, GA 30084
online: *http://www.moe.cc.emory.edu/~rlchurc/bca.html*

Magazines

Sour Mug
#1 Windyridge
Mendota, MN 55150

Living

with a

part two

Bulldog

chapter 4

Bringing Your **Bulldog** Home

Before you actually bring a puppy home, ask yourself if you really are ready to make a commitment of ten to fifteen years. There is the cost of food and medical care, and most importantly the investment of time. Do you have time every day to share with your pet or will this just be an hour-a-day relationship or worse yet, a few hours on the weekend? Will you be able to let your Bulldog share your life, live in your home and sleep by your chair as you read or watch TV in the evening? You must also consider grooming responsibilities. There is bathing (rarely), almost daily brushing, regular nail trimming—these tasks take time (and money if done by professionals).

Hopefully, everyone in the household agrees on wanting a Bulldog, because sooner or later each person will have to care for the dog.

Does dog hair on your navy blue suit or dress drive you up the wall, or are you willing to change your wardrobe to colors that do not show dog hair as readily?

We all like nice clean houses, but are you one who must have everything immaculate? The hair on your clothes also falls on the floor and furniture. This is not to say that Bulldogs shed excessively, but all dogs do shed. Bulldogs are shorthaired and with regular brushing, shedding really is not a problem unless you are one of those people who wants everything perfect. If you are, a dog (any dog) would interfere with your way of life. It is better that these questions be answered before you get a puppy.

In spite of all of these potential problems and duties, you want a Bulldog!

Selecting Your Puppy

Before you can bring a Bulldog home, you must find one. Bulldogs are not a prolific breed. Compared to other breeds, Bulldog litters are usually small and many females fail to conceive. The demand for puppies generally is greater than the supply!

Have patience! Your Bulldog is worth waiting for. Rarely are Bulldogs found in pet shops. Since the supply is limited and demand high, a reputable breeder has no need to use a third party to market his or her pups.

What is a reputable breeder? First and foremost, he or she must have integrity and care about the dogs. How are the dogs housed? Are they clean? How do they react to their owner? Judging by the number of dogs, is this obviously a commercial project? Some commercial projects are acceptable, but they are the exception rather than the rule.

A breeder with a "one dog" backyard setup can be wrong, too. It really depends upon the operator in charge and his motivation. Are money and profits the

priorities or is there truly an interest in the welfare of
the dogs? To be a successful, happy breeder, you must
truly enjoy breeding and raising puppies, because it is
hard work!

A breeder who really cares about his dogs will screen
the potential buyer just as carefully as he, the breeder,
is being screened. As a buyer, be truthful.

A pet-quality pup will probably cost less money than
a potential show dog—but will not win in the showring or produce quality pups. He will have just as
much love and companionship to give as his blue-
ribbon brothers.

*All puppies are
cute, but it is
most important
that the one you
choose is healthy
and happy.*

Of course, you want to be sure your pup is registered
with AKC, or at least the registration has been applied
for. Accept none of this "he is purebred but we just
never registered his mother," or "his father is eligible
but has not been registered." The owner (if reputable)
of the male would not breed an unregistered female
and vice versa. If you are unfortunate enough to
find yourself in this situation, even though the puppies
are inexpensive, are *so* cute (all puppies are cute) and
seem healthy and happy—STOP! Let your head control your heart and march your feet away quickly.
Registration, like a trademark, gives some assurance of

the final product. Only the very experienced breeder can detect crossbreeding in tiny puppies. The breeder should give you at least a three generation pedigree as well as a health and shot record.

You should be allowed to take the pup or adult dog to a veterinarian of your choice within seventy-two hours for a health and physical exam. If the veterinarian finds anything wrong—i.e., heart murmur, cryptorchid, etc.—the seller or breeder should take the dog back.

I repeat that a pup is a ten to fifteen year commitment, so your entire family should want the pup. Because the Bulldog will become a family member, everyone should realize the puppy will be bringing home all his good traits, as well as some not so good (e.g., snoring).

Most Bulldog breeders are sincere, honest people. They care about the welfare of their dogs and want only the best for you and the dog. Take time to find the puppy that is just what you have been dreaming about and enjoy the love and devotion that are complete and nonjudgmental.

How do you find a breeder, if you do not have personal knowledge of one or know someone who has a Bulldog? Ask the local veterinarian, boarding kennels, pet supply stores or owners and breeders of other breeds. Answer ads in papers, but carefully check out the advertiser before you purchase your puppy this way. Write to the American Kennel Club and ask for its list of breeders, or write to the Bulldog Club of America, which will direct you to breeders in your part of the country.

Surely, one or more of these sources will be able to give you leads to more than one breeder. Early spring is probably the best time to look for a puppy and early summer is the best time to get a puppy. The supply of puppies is usually greater in the spring of the year. Most animals' breeding cycles, like the renewal of plant life, begin in the spring. Also, it is much easier to housetrain a puppy in warm weather. Neither you nor the puppy want to trek out-of-doors in cold weather so the puppy can take care of his bodily functions (especially in the middle of the night).

You have decided you do want a Bulldog. You have read the standard and you have found a nice litter of puppies bred by a reputable breeder. These puppies are or will be AKC registered. You have seen their mother and have been given the history of their father.

WHAT AGE?

Bulldogs are good with children, but 8-week-old puppies and babies under 3 years are not a good combination. Neither is mature enough to comprehend the limitations of the other. If there are children under 3 years of age in your family, I suggest you look for a puppy at least 6 months old, or a young adult dog. It is not true that a pup must grow up with a child to accept the child. A little time and a little patience and even an older dog can be taught. However, a dog that has spent his entire life in a kennel may not be a good or happy house dog.

WHAT COLOR?

You had your heart set on a white puppy but there are no white puppies. Should you look further for the white puppy? If the only thing that is preventing you from selecting one puppy from a litter is color, then I suggest you select the next best puppy. By that I mean the one that pleases you most in this particular litter and that the breeder will sell. Color really is not important, and soon you will have forgotten you ever wanted a white one as the brindle one (or the brown one or the black one) finds its way into your heart.

MALE OR FEMALE?

Should you get a male or a female? Because you will be sure to neuter your pet Bulldog, males and females make equally good pets. Neutering prevents many problems as your Bulldog grows older.

So What Is Important?

In a few words, select an outgoing, vigorous, playful puppy regardless of color or sex.

If you were planning to use your puppy for breeding, then the number and quality of champions in his pedigree would be a selling point. But your pup is not going to be a champion, so champion parents and the number of champions in his family tree are not important. It is important that he is AKC registered, healthy and a good specimen of the breed.

When to Bring Your Puppy Home

Select a time when you will be at home for several days. Your puppy needs to get to know you; to become acclimated to her new home and crate and to get comfortable with her daily schedule of walks, playtime and perhaps her new food (don't change food, unless absolutely necessary, for several days, and then change gradually).

Your puppy needs time to explore her new home and to get used to her new family.

She needs some free time just to explore. She needs to be held and loved. Just imagine yourself in her place. Your puppy can't talk and she can't really understand what you are saying. Everything is new and different. It takes time, but the time that is spent now will help her learn to trust you and be a happy, confident animal living a wonderful life.

Holidays

It is not wise to get a new puppy at holiday time. First, the house is certainly not on any kind of a schedule. Christmas trees are fascinating but certainly a no-no. Wrapping paper, packages, pins, ribbons are all likely

49

to be on the floor; these can not only be dangerous for your puppy, but he may also upset some family members with his explorations into their packages. Don't tempt him. A puppy is a baby, and he will get tired of being handled and played with by many different people. If you must get or take him at holiday time, then be sure he has a crate in a nice, quiet, warm place. Do not allow everyone to hold him and don't be guilty of showing him to everyone who comes to visit. Remember, he is a confused, bewildered baby.

If you have gotten an adult dog, the same plan should be followed. He may be grown, but he doesn't understand why he has a new home or where his former owner is. He needs time to bond with you and feel safe and wanted.

What Kind of Home Does Your Puppy Need?

A fenced-in area where the puppy will be safe, and which the neighbors accept, is almost a must. Just as you need a little private time in your bathroom to contemplate the problems of the world, so does the puppy need a little private time to run about off-lead and smell all the wonderful, interesting scents about him. He needs to sit in the sun, watch the birds, get a fresh drink of water and maybe take a little snooze. A concrete run will do, but a little green grass to stretch out on is heaven. This does not eliminate the need to go for a walk, but it certainly makes housetraining and caring for toilet needs simpler. A pooper-scooper is also necessary to help keep the area clean. A clean area will not attract flies or nasty remarks from the neighbors. Check carefully for any poisonous weeds, shrubs or plants.

Do not spray the dog run with insecticides or herbicides. Some of these chemicals may damage the dog's immune system. We do fertilize and spray our lawn for grubs, but we are very careful to keep the dogs and people off the grass for at least seventy-two hours and have not had any problems.

Necessary Equipment

There are certain supplies needed to help you and the puppy prepare for a satisfying and long life together.

COLLARS AND LEASHES

Personally I prefer a show leash or a lightweight chain, choke collar and leash. They adjust to the size of the dog's neck and head and are *only* worn when going for a walk. This kind of lead eliminates the use of a leather or nylon collar, but without a collar there is no place to put a license or identifying tags. Tags are no longer necessary if you choose the tattoo or microchip route. Ask your veterinarian about these options. Teach the dog that the collar and leash mean walk or grooming time.

Bulldogs appreciate safe outdoor play areas.

I have always been somewhat apprehensive of the dog wearing a collar all of the time. If the dog gets out and somehow gets "hooked up" because of his collar, there could be problems. But if your decision is a collar to be worn all the time, then a narrow leather collar is best. Do not use a spike collar or harness. A harness is totally unnecessary and if you try to use it for control, you're likely to find your dog will only pull harder on his leash. Use a light choke collar to teach control, but *do not* leave this collar on when he isn't being walked.

51

To the naive, the spike collar is the symbol of the Bulldog. To the true bulldogger, it represents the awful cruelty of the dog's beginnings—something we would rather forget.

Collars and leads can be purchased at pet stores as well as many other places. Using the information given, get the one you like best. While we are discussing collars and leashes, never chain your Bulldog to the clothesline or a post in the ground. He is vulnerable to anyone or anything that happens along. He can get tangled in the chain, the sun can move about and he can get too hot and die.

BABY GATES

You should decide before you bring your puppy home just how much freedom she will have in the house. Will she be free to go anyplace or will boundaries be established?

It is very difficult for a dog to observe a nonexistent barrier that keeps her from someplace she wants to go. (Difficult for me, too!) If certain parts of your home are to be off limits, there are good, attractive baby gates on the market. Some are built so there is a gate within the gate and all you have to do is open this gate when you need to go through it. This type is probably the most practical.

Crate Training

With a small puppy, it is best to confine him to specific areas until he is completely "house-trained." The ideal plan is to have a place where he can be confined in the kitchen or utility area, someplace where he is a part of the family. He could come into the family room for a short time, and under constant supervision, right after he has done his "duty" outside. As he grows and matures, he will be allowed more freedom.

The easiest and most effective way to confine a puppy is to get a metal crate at least 24" wide × 36" long × 26" high. Place it where the puppy is to sleep; make sure this area is warm and free of drafts. Confine the puppy, except for definite play- and exercise time, for the first few days. Leave the door open when the puppy is out so he can return at will.

IS A CRATE A JAIL FOR YOUR PET?

Crates serve many functions for pet owners. Many people use a cage to housebreak their puppy or adult dog. This is an excellent method because it allows you to train your pet more rapidly and with less trauma, be it mental or physical. They can also be used for pets that are destructive while the owner is away. They make travel with your pet much safer for you and the animal.

If the owner is away, the pet may be caged for several hours; many pet owners wonder if this is cruel or inhumane. In my experience it is not. In fact, in most cases training done in this manner is less traumatic to the pet than other training methods. Most pets do not resent a crate, but rather find it to be a safe and secure retreat. Many people using a crate for housebreaking will see their pet laying in the crate with the door open when they are tired and want someplace quiet to sleep. At other times, when the hustle and bustle of the home is reaching a high point, the pet may voluntarily retire to her crate with a bone to chew on. I believe that cages and crates are one of the very best training tools. Don't feel guilty about using one.

FOOD AND WATER DISHES

There are pans that clip on the sides of the crate for food and water. The pup should *always* have fresh water available.

Pans of stainless steel or other metal are fine out of the crate, but heavy plastic or "crock" type are best. Some Bulldogs enjoy picking up their pans and tossing them about after they have finished eating. Scattered food is nothing more than a mess—but spilled water cannot satisfy thirst.

TOYS

Soft toys and "chew" bones make life a little more interesting when the dog is alone. Hard rubber bones, and *real* sterilized bones can be purchased from a pet shop, and they are safe and acceptable. Some soft toys are safe. Check the squeaker; if it is metal, it must be taken out or the toy must be left in the store. (The metal squeaker can choke.)

I make my own soft toys. A child's tube sock stuffed full with strips of nylon panty hose or any strips of well-worn rags and then sewed shut is an ideal toy. Our dogs will grab this, throw it up, try to catch it, tease, etc. When it is dirty, toss it into the washer. Washed, rinsed, dried and it becomes new again, or if it is worn out, toss it. Little money has been involved. Be sure any balls are too large for the dog to swallow and not of foam rubber that can break off into chunks.

Playing with your puppy bolsters his confidence and coordination.

As for bones to chew, I go to the butcher and ask him to saw beef leg bones (marrow bones) 5 to 7 inches long. Put these bones in the oven and bake at 300° to 350° for about three hours. Loosen the marrow and give the bone to the dog to chew. He will have to chew these bones on the linoleum floor or in his crate until they are clean. The dogs seem to enjoy these home-baked bones more than the "commercial" products. From time to time I renew the flavor of the bone by filling the center with hamburger and garlic powder, wrapping the bone in aluminum foil and baking it for two to three hours. I loosen the hamburger and it's like a new bone. These do not get smelly. They are safe and the dogs like them. Dogs enjoy beef hide or rawhide chews, but the Bulldog has the ability to soften these and the result may be a dog who chokes on softened pieces. If you are going to use these you must be present when your dog is enjoying his treat. This includes the smoked "pigs'" ears. It would seem that the chew hooves (smoked or natural cow hooves) would be safe, but again, although the dog really enjoys the "hooves," his jaws are so strong that after chewing for a time he can break off sharp pieces that are as dangerous as any bone that splinters.

Do not give your dog an old shoe to use as a toy. Then any shoe—new and never worn, or old and unwearable—is the same to the dog and sooner or later your brand new shoe becomes a toy. But I must tell you that the above isn't always correct. Dandy, at 3 months of age, claimed a well-worn sneaker as his own and kept it throughout his lifetime. (He never took another shoe—the exception to the rule.)

Sometimes this precious possession was in the middle of the living room floor and sometimes only Dandy knew where *his* shoe was. If we had a visitor and Dandy approved, he would get his shoe and present it to the visitor. If for some reason the visitor was unacceptable, the shoe would be immediately hidden. This illustrates that a dog cares about his things, has his own standards and is possessive. As time goes on, a puppy grows up and, like children, seems to collect various possessions. Safety is the watchword.

Puppyproofing Your Home

The Bulldog should be trained to respect her home (your house). But there are a few things that need to be done. All cleaning materials, bleach, soap, ammonia, etc., must be on high shelves and behind closed doors, *especially* antifreeze. For some reason most dogs like the taste of antifreeze. Fertilizer (liquid and dry), insecticides and motor oil should be kept up high or behind closed doors. Use care with your own prescriptions; store them carefully and safely.

Puppies especially are fascinated by extension and lamp cords. Chewing these could result in electrocution of the dog or a fire. Bulldog puppies are not as destructive as some other breeds and generally do not chew on furniture unless they are bored. If the pup is to be left alone where lamp cords or extension cords are, then the cords must be disconnected and put away. However, if you are going to be with him, leave the cords in their regular places. He must be taught to leave the cords alone. This requires time and persistence. Give him a stern *NO* every time he goes near the cords. After all, you share this house and, in time, he will understand that certain things are *NO!* Every time he approaches anything that is off limits—*NO!* But praise him highly when he is a good boy. Dogs learn what they can and what they can't do. Our Cleo never gets on the davenport or any furniture in the living room, but sleeps on the davenport in my son's part of the house. She knows she may sleep with me on my bed, but not on my davenport.

Protect your possessions by puppyproofing your home!

All of these words may tend to discourage you—but just remember a puppy is just like a human baby—he needs to be taught, he needs to learn and he needs to be protected. Your reward is a wonderful companion for all of the life of your Bulldog!

Choosing a Veterinarian

Finally, before you bring your puppy home, select a veterinarian to care for her health. Select the veterinarian as you would your own private physician or pediatrician. Not only his veterinary knowledge, but also his availability, should be considered. Since your Bulldog is not going to be shown or used for breeding, spaying the female should be considered. This prevents the twice a year need to confine and watch her very closely during her heat periods. Also, statistics prove that breast cancer (yes, dogs have cancer) and pyometra (uterine infection) are less likely to occur in spayed females. Neutered males are less aggressive and less likely to "mark" the furniture (although this is rarely a problem with Bulldogs).

Discuss the care of your dog with your veterinarian; he is better able to advise you than the next-door neighbor or the man down the street.

5

Feeding
Your Bulldog

Most Bulldogs believe that everything that is chewable can be eaten. Many Bulldogs even like fresh fruits, especially oranges and watermelon. I do not recommend that he be given these fruits freely or frequently, but every once in a while, smile, give him a small piece of watermelon and watch him chomp and enjoy. So, the problem of feeding a Bulldog isn't finding something he will eat, but searching through the myriad brands, formulas and consistencies to find what is best for him and readily available.

Dog food is a lucrative business. Big sums of money are spent on advertising and developing foods that are palatable and healthy. On the practical side of the coin, the cost of these foods must be reasonable and within the reach of the average consumer.

Dogs, like people, are individuals, and their metabolic rates vary. There is a dog food made specially for every stage in a dog's life, from puppyhood to old age. There are also different formulas made for the active dog, for the dog under stressful conditions and for the couch potato.

Where to Buy Food

Today there are large supermarket stores just for pets. Almost everything you could want or need, including many brands of food, is available in these stores. You are fortunate if you have access to one of these. Supermarket groceries carry many of the well-advertised brands. If your dog is on special food prescribed by your veterinarian, he usually has the food available.

In rural areas, animal feed stores carrying specific brands of animal feed generally carry the same brands of dog food.

Protein

Probably the most important element in dog food is protein. The protein in puppy food is 27 to 30 percent; 27 to 30 percent protein would be too much for the old dog or the couch potato. The percentage of protein is important, but also the availability and quality of the protein must be high. The availability of the protein concerns the dog's ability to utilize the food. When reading labels you will find a food that contains 27 to 30 percent protein and is three or four dollars cheaper than another brand with the same percentage of protein. Quality is probably the reason. To ensure you are getting the right amount of nutrients for your dog, the easiest and best thing to do may be to buy a premium dog food made for your dog's stage of life and activity level. You can ask your veterinarian for further advice.

Reading Labels

Dog food manufacturers are required to list the contents of the food on the container. Learning to read and understand these labels is important. The ingredients are listed in descending order by weight. When you read the contents notice if the meat (protein) is listed as just meat (chicken, for example) or meat by-products? If it's simply chicken, then only the meat of the chicken will be used. If it's listed as chicken by-products, any and all parts of the chicken are used. Dog foods containing by-products will be less costly, and in many cases will be as satisfactory as the meat-only formulas.

Read dog food labels so you know that what your dog is eating is nutritious.

The guaranteed analysis tells the percentage of protein, fat, carbohydrates, fiber and moisture in the food but does not indicate the quality of each. There is also a list of the various vitamins and minerals as well as the caloric content. The daily amount to feed according to the breed and size of the dog, as well as his age and activity, is also suggested. This is a lot of information in a small space, but it must be read, understood and evaluated if you are to get the best for your dog and for your dollar.

There are three types of food: dry (kibbles and chunks), canned and semimoist. The dry food usually is the best buy, as you are not paying for moisture or metal containers. In addition, the hard food helps to keep the dog's teeth clean by scraping tartar off the teeth as the dog chews.

The moisture in the canned food is a mixture of broth and blood, two flavors especially relished by dogs. Try mixing a can of food and an amount of dry food equal to three cans. This is a good mixture that the dog will enjoy and eat. No food is wasted and there are fewer cans to wash and recycle.

The semimoist food is well-accepted by dogs, but it contains preservatives, as well as artificial colors. The artificial colors only make the food more attractive to the buyer. The dog doesn't care: He is color blind.

Treats

And then there are treats: treats of all shapes and sizes, and treats that are more than just treats. Some help keep the teeth free of tartar, some have very high caloric content and some are just fun to eat. Read the labels, applying the same criteria as you would to regular dog food. Treats are special, but they should still be good for your dog. Treats should not be used as a steady diet. They are too expensive! Use a treat as a reward for good behavior or as a special time of day treat (i.e., bedtime or as you are leaving the house).

PEOPLE FOOD

If an occasional treat from the table is available, use it. It seems to me that the dog not only enjoys the treat but somehow gets a message that he is special, and he is! These treats can be bits of meat, gravy, even green beans. A piece of cheese is wonderful, and a piece of toast at breakfast time is a great way to start the day. Don't make table scraps a routine; make them very special. For a balance of nutrition, it is best if they comprise 10 percent or less of the pet's total daily food intake. Treats from the table should never be offered in such amounts that your pet avoids his regular food.

No-Nos

Some scraps, however, should be avoided, such as rich fatty foods and chicken and pork chop bones. Do not offer your dog highly spiced food or chocolate. If you mix an egg in with your dog's meal, make sure it's cooked. If fed in excess, fatty foods such as bacon grease can cause diarrhea and trigger other, more severe digestive upsets. Poultry and pork bones can lodge in the intestinal tract with serious results.

Feeding Times

The adult dog may be fed once daily. However, if you are comfortable dividing and feeding twice daily it is probably better for the dog, especially for Bulldogs, because some of them will vomit bile if their stomachs are empty for too long a time. Remember to feed only part of the day's allowance at each feeding. I have found that the big meal should be offered in the morning and then the same food, but a smaller amount, should be given at night.

If you have been given antibiotics to administer to your dog, either by mouth or injection, add cottage cheese or yogurt to his diet while he is taking the medication.

Puppy Regimen

The above is general information for the adult dog and you have brought home an 8-week-old puppy. He is getting his puppy teeth, his gums are swollen, his mouth is sore and he misses his brothers and sisters. I know the puppy food formula is supposed to be complete and I'm sure it is, but all babies need milk. I've used the following formula for years and found it a decided plus for Bulldog puppies.

> 1 can (12 oz.) regular Carnation milk
>
> 1 cup (8 oz.) cottage cheese
>
> 10 drops lactose-free milk

Put these ingredients in a blender and mix until smooth. This should be allowed to stand in refrigeration for four to six hours before using, but can be used immediately. The lactose-free milk contains enzymes that help the pup tolerate milk.

I soak the puppy kibbles in warm water (just enough to cover) and then put them into a blender and blend until smooth. Use two parts of the softened kibbles to one part of the milk formula and feed as much as the puppy wants, unless he is a glutton and overeats. If he gets diarrhea or eats until his tummy is overfull, then rationing becomes the order of the day until the quantity of food needed to keep the puppy growing and satisfied is reached, but not exceeded.

Puppies should be a little chubby. Puppy fat means your pup is well-nourished and growing. Eight-week-old puppies should be fed five times daily using the moistened kibbles and milk formula. If your puppy doesn't eat all the food you have given him after fifteen to twenty minutes, take it away, but leave a small pan of the dry kibbles available for him to chomp on. *Always* have fresh water available.

When the puppy is 4 months old, reduce the number of times he is fed to four times daily. Continue this schedule until he is 6 months old. From 6 to 10 months feed three times daily, then twice daily until he is 1 year old. After that, once each day, unless you are more comfortable with the twice daily feeding.

Supplementation

Added vitamins are not necessary unless the puppy is not growing. If he isn't growing, or if stools vary from constipation to diarrhea, see your veterinarian to ask about supplementation.

Sometimes, when a pup is 11 to 15 weeks old, his ears will droop. Generally this means his calcium intake is low, due to rapid growth, and loss of his puppy teeth and growth of his adult teeth. It may be necessary to give extra calcium for a few weeks, or just more plain cottage cheese. I usually discontinue the carnation milk–cottage cheese formula at 6 months and give one cup of cottage cheese daily.

Fresh Water

Fresh water must always be available. There is no moisture in the dry food and your puppy must have water available. Check the water bowl several times a day, especially when you have puppies who seem to like playing in their water dishes, and rinse and refill as necessary.

Different Food for Different Stages

As time passes and your dog gets older and lazier, her diet must change to fit her slower lifestyle. Lower calories, less protein and a smaller amount will be necessary. The older dog formula manufactured by a leading dog food company should take these nutritional considerations into account. Dog food companies are doing an excellent job of providing the right food, so take advantage of it!

Keep plenty of fresh water available for your Bulldog at all times.

As long as your dog is healthy, do not make changes. If your dog or puppy's coat is bright and shiny, her eyes clear, stools formed and muscles firm, don't change her food. Dogs don't tire of the same diet day after day—just owners!

chapter 6

Grooming
Your Bulldog

Bulldogs really enjoy being groomed (except for nail trimming), and many especially enjoy taking baths. If you use the bathtub to bathe your Bulldog, be sure to close your bathroom door tightly when taking your bath or you may have him trying to share the tub with you!

The Bulldog has a smooth, short coat and is naturally a reasonably clean dog. Because of his short coat many people think grooming is not needed. Not true. The cost of having a professional groomer clip, pluck, trim or shape is an expense you will not have, but there is more to grooming than elaborate coat care.

Grooming should be regular and routine—just as your own personal grooming is. Don't wait until your puppy has grown up. Start now. Stand the puppy on a bench or table, or any flat surface that is the best height for your comfort. Assure the puppy that he isn't being punished and this is a special time just for him.

Check for any bare spots in his coat, or skin lesions, and note the sheen. Are his eyes clear and free of discharge? Is his nose soft and free of crust? Are the insides of his ears smooth or is the skin rough, flaky and inflamed? Note his feet—are they swollen, especially between his toes? This seems like a lot of checking but before you realize, it will become a regular habit to observe all these points and you will immediately be aware of any abnormalities that can indicate potential problems.

Dogs need to be groomed regularly from an early age.

Brushing

First on the daily grooming ritual will be brushing. How much and how long will depend upon the condition of the coat. Your dog's coat is a good barometer of her health. Is the shedding minimal or is it excessive? If it is not seasonal excess, then there must be another reason—Stress? Worms? Fleas? Diet change? All these and more can cause excess shedding, and only your veterinarian can truly make a diagnosis.

Only seasonal shedding will right itself. Excessive loss of hair for other reasons must be treated. Excessive shedding leaves Bulldog hair on the furniture, on your clothes, in fact everywhere, and Bulldog hair is difficult to get off—it sticks!

A small pumice stone (2"× 4") helps remove the dead hair during heavy shedding. Brush with the stone in the direction of the hair. Complete the grooming with a slicker brush or grooming glove, both of which can be purchased at a pet supply store.

When the shedding is normal, a daily brushing with a slicker brush or glove should be adequate. Loose hair, dandruff, and dirt will be removed, leaving the coat bright and shiny and the hair follicles stimulated.

Ears

Check the ears next. Are they being carried properly ("rose" ears are the desirable shape)? Around 12 weeks of age, when puppies begin to get their adult teeth, the ears may droop. Using ear cement (available at pet stores), glue the ear in the "rose" position. The breeder of your puppy should be able to help you

Brushing should be a part of your Bulldog's daily routine.

the first time. Also, when you pet your puppy, always stroke from front to back on his head in order to maintain the proper ear position. (This is just a puppy problem.)

Observe the inside of the ears. Insert a cotton swab (be sure cotton is securely anchored on the swab) a short distance into the canal. Is there foul smelling discharge on the swab? Does the canal appear red or swollen? Is your dog shaking his head or rubbing his ears? These symptoms may indicate ear infection, which requires professional intervention. If there is little or no debris on the swab, all is well and a weekly inspection is enough. Use different swabs for each ear. Warm mineral oil on the swab will help remove the dry, flaky skin.

If your dog's nose is dry and rough, use some of the mineral oil on his nose.

Those Hard to Reach Places

*Ears need to be
inspected weekly
for signs of infec-
tion—discharge,
redness and
swelling.*

The Bulldog's face covered with wrinkles is certainly his trademark. But this is a trademark that requires daily care to keep the dog comfortable. Mild soap, a soap that you would use on your own face, warm water and a soft cloth should be used to wash the wrinkles. If your dog has a heavy nose wrinkle, lift it carefully and wash underneath, rinse and dry. If it is especially dirty and inflamed, treat it with a medicated powder, baby powder or cornstarch. It may be necessary to wash the wrinkles more than once daily. Use care and cau-

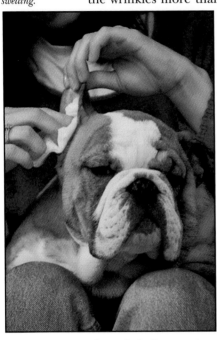

tion with powder. Be sure not to get any into the dog's eyes or nose and be sure it does not contain poisonous substances. Boric acid is a poison!

While you are cleaning the wrinkles on the dog's face, there are two more areas unique to Bulldogs that must be cleaned.

Most breeds of dogs care for their own personal hygiene by licking themselves. Not the Bulldog! The female cannot reach her vulva to keep it clean. So after all wrinkles are washed, wash Lady Bulldog's vulva (not inside), rinse, dry and powder if inflamed. If there is inflammation, watch closely for discharge or odor. If this persists, a visit to the veterinarian is in order.

Mr. Bulldog either cannot or will not take care of his own personal hygiene, so check the inside of his hind legs. If there is evidence of dirt or discharge, wash thoroughly with soap and water (include his penis and outside foreskin), rinse and dry. As with the female, if inflammation is present or discharge has a foul odor, have your veterinarian check his condition.

Yes, the Bulldog does have some special problems, but he will never embarrass you by caring for his personal hygiene in the presence of someone you want to impress.

Finally, one more area is a Bulldog problem. If you selected a puppy that has a "spiked" or loosely kinked tail that "wags freely and easily," then you and your dog will not have to contend with this problem. If his tail is tight to his body, twisted and curled almost in knots or is totally absent, then regular inspection and cleansing is the order of the day. Cover your finger with a soft, warm, soapy cloth and get under the tail. You will discover there is loose hair and flaking skin and other debris under the tail where it emerges from the body. Cleanse carefully and gently—dry and powder using whatever you have used for wrinkles. Follow this same procedure in the knots and twists. If there is no tail there is usually an indentation where the tail should be. This indentation will contain dead hair, dandruff, etc. This, too, must be cleaned. Keeping this area clean and dry will help to prevent infection. A severely infected tail may have to be removed, which is expensive and painful. Prevention may be a nuisance, but it is less expensive for you, and certainly less painful for the dog, than treating an infection.

Eyes

Check for excessive tearing or swollen lids. The lids may be turned in, a condition called entropion. Unfortunately this may require surgical intervention. See your veterinarian!

Toenails

All dogs living the cultured, domestic, protected existence of today have to have their nails trimmed. Nail trimming should begin almost immediately after birth. At least every week the white part or tip of the nail should be trimmed. The only problem is that Bulldogs' nails are black. Even the tips are black. Because of this it will be hard to see where the quick (the end of the blood supply to the nail) is. The best thing to do is remove just the tips and clip more frequently. For clipping you will need a nail scissors or a guillotine type clipper, or you can buy a grinder. This takes more time, but if the dog is cooperative, there is less danger of grinding too short. Start as soon as you get your puppy. At first trim just the very tips so you do not cause any pain; if you are lucky the dog will accept this procedure reluctantly. But you can get it done. I've only had one dog who would present his paws to have his nails trimmed.

If you cannot trim the nails, then either your veterinarian or a professional groomer will have to be employed. You *must* keep nails trimmed, or your dog's feet will become misshapen. A daily *long* walk on a rough surface (sidewalks work well) will make nail trimming necessary less often.

Frequent nail trims will keep the job simple and easy to do at home.

As a pet owner, you may shy away from trimming your pet's nails. Perhaps you are afraid you will cause your pet pain or bleeding. This is possible, but in the absence of proper care the nails overgrow and can painfully break or split and even curl back into the foot. Nail trimming is easy if done on a regular basis. When you trim your own finger or toenails, you understand you are only trimming away excess dead cells. The same is true when you trim your dog's toenails. You only need to know how to recognize the dead portion of her nails. You may feel this is harder to do in pets with black or pigmented nails, because you won't be able to see the quick. Make the cut just ouside the hooklike projection on the underside of the nail.

If the nail starts to bleed, it is not serious and you can use styptic powder to quickly stop it. Remember, it's better to trim a small amount on a regular basis than to try to remove large portions.

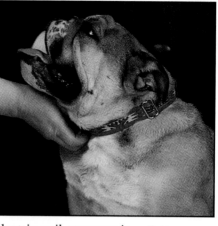

Either a guillotine type or a scissors type nail trimmer is necessary. Either is satisfactory and whichever you find is best for you is the one to use. If time and money are not a problem, a cordless or electric nail groomer is very good. This instrument grinds the nails and lessens the chance of getting them too short. If the dog is cooperative, this is the best and safest method. An electric groomer costs about $50 but lasts a lifetime.

Keeping your Bulldog well-groomed shows him that you care about his well-being.

Mouth and Gums

An inspection of the mouth and teeth every few weeks is wise. Inflamed, pale or bleeding gums will call for a visit to the veterinarian.

Bath Time

Most Bulldogs really enjoy a bath. Your bathtub is probably the best place. If she is introduced to a bath when she is a puppy and easily handled, she will enjoy the bath throughout her life. Use a mild soap, baby soap or non-medicated soap for the dog. A dog's skin is more sensitive than yours, so do not use harsh soaps, medicated soaps, or flea soaps unless ordered by your veterinarian. Be careful, and avoid getting it in her eyes, ears or nose. Wash her face as you do each morning and bathe the rest of the dog starting at the shoulders and going to the tail. Rinse well.

Let the dog shake off the water, then lift her out of tub and finish drying her off with a towel. I don't like using a hair dryer, the heat of which tends to dry the coat. Bulldogs do not need frequent baths, but instead need bathing only when they are dirty. Frequent brushing will do much more for a healthy, shiny coat than bathing.

Bulldogs enjoy grooming because they are people dogs and enjoy anything that involves attention from those they love. Grooming is an exercise in observation and prevention providing a healthy, happy, clean dog. I have recommended daily grooming, but if your skills of observation are keen and your dog does not have any problems, it is no sin to reduce the frequency to two or three times weekly.

chapter 7

Keeping Your Bulldog Healthy

The first step to a healthy Bulldog is to get a healthy puppy, born of healthy parents and with healthy siblings. The next step is to get a good veterinarian. Select your veterinarian *before* you bring your puppy home. This veterinarian should have some knowledge of the Bulldog, the idiosyncrasies and special needs of the breed, and be available when

needed. Some veterinarians close up shop on weekends and holidays and direct their clients to an emergency center. This really is not the best arrangement. The clinic may be above reproach and provide excellent care, but the dog's records, a valuable diagnostic tool, are in one place, the dog in another; time is lost and treatment is delayed.

Have an appointment with the selected veterinarian within seventy-two hours after taking possession of the puppy. Take all the data (immunizations, worm checks, diet) given to you by the breeder for evaluation and plans for future care. All this information will help the veterinarian establish a schedule to prevent problems rather than treat problems after they develop.

Vaccinations

Generally your puppy will be given a series of shots starting at about 6 weeks of age and being repeated every three to four weeks until he is 6 months of age, and then annually for the remainder of his life. A vaccination schedule will be determined by your veterinarian according to his experience and knowledge. I would caution you not to be penny-wise and pound foolish and skip any shots prescribed. Prevention is far less costly than treatment, and rarely has complications. Treatment has many! Distemper, Hepatitis, Leptospirosis, Parvo and Corona usually are combined in one shot, which is repeated annually after the initial series of puppy shots. This, of course, is your veterinarian's decision. I also urge you to keep a complete vaccination program current. A complete vaccination program is money well-spent; your dog will need fewer trips to the veterinarian. What are these immunizations for?

YOUR PUPPY'S VACCINES

Vaccines are given to prevent your dog from getting an infectious disease like canine distemper or rabies. Vaccines are the ultimate preventive medicine: They're given before your dog ever gets the disease so as to protect him from the disease. That's why it is necessary for your dog to be vaccinated routinely. Puppy vaccines start at 8 weeks of age for the five-in-one DHLPP vaccine and are given every three to four weeks until the puppy is 16 months old. Your veterinarian will put your puppy on a proper schedule and will remind you when to bring in your dog for shots.

RABIES

Vaccination against rabies is essential and, as far as we know, compulsory in every state. Rabies is caused by a virus and is transmitted by the saliva of an infected mammal (domestic or wild). Once the symptoms develop, rabies is usually fatal.

My husband was a veterinarian with a country practice (large domestic animals). In the early 1940s he experienced a rabies epidemic that they believed was caused by a cat that went across the country biting anything in its path. Fortunately, no people were bitten, but hogs, a few cattle, as well as dogs were involved before the cat was captured. At that time vaccination for rabies was

not compulsory. Today, domestic animals are rarely infected, but rabies still crops up in wild animals occasionally.

One of the classic symptoms of a rabid animal is behavioral change. A normally shy animal may attack, while a usually aggressive one will run away. If you see a dog or wild animal acting strangely, call the authorities. Do not attempt to handle the animal. Keep your dog's rabies vaccination current according to your veterinarian's advice.

DISTEMPER

Distemper is a nasty viral disease that, years ago, would wipe out entire kennels of dogs! The respiratory system, neurological system, gastro-intestinal system—in fact the whole dog—were involved and complications were so severe that death was a blessing. The vaccination for this dreadful disease has all but eliminated it.

Discuss a vaccination program with your veterinarian and stick to it.

HEPATITIS

"Hepatic" means liver and "itis" refers to inflammation. Hepatitis is a viral disease of the liver passed from one infected dog to another through saliva, stools and urine. The symptoms are fever, discharge from nose and eyes, loss of appetite, clay colored stools and diarrhea. Vaccination is a must!

LEPTOSPIROSIS

Leptospirosis is a bacterial disease and is easier to treat than viral diseases. But don't let this be an excuse to skip vaccination. Although the disease is rare and it can be treated, recovery is slow and even after recovery, the dog may be a carrier and infect nonvaccinated dogs. Immunization is simple, inexpensive and necessary.

PARVOVIRUS/CORONAVIRUS

These are viral diseases that are transmitted through the feces of an infected dog. They are easily carried on the hair and feet of a dog or shoes of anyone who has been where infected dogs were. Both are highly contagious at all ages but young dogs and pups are most susceptible. Symptoms are fever, vomiting and diarrhea (the stools have a peculiar, fetid, foul odor).

Treatment is only symptomatic and not too successful. The terms "parvo" and "corona" strike fear into the hearts of dog owners, especially if their dog's vaccinations are not current.

Make a note of your Bulldog's normal behavior so you'll be able to recognize potential problems when they appear.

KENNEL COUGH (BORDATELLA)

This is one more vaccination your veterinarian may recommend. Kennel cough is highly contagious and, just like the flu in people, it produces runny noses, inflamed eyes, a dry hacking cough and sometimes a sore throat. It is really a mixture of viruses and bacteria. The vaccine is reasonably effective, but unlike the other diseases mentioned, vaccination is not absolutely necessary. Let your veterinarian advise you on this.

Internal Parasites

HEARTWORM

As the name implies, the worm lives inside the dog's heart and in the adjacent large blood vessels. Heartworm is preventable and treatable, but if not treated, and sometimes if treated, it is fatal, so prevention is the order of the day. The disease is transmitted from dog to dog by mosquitoes. Once heartworms are established in the heart, they will reproduce and the resultant larvae (microfilariae) will circulate throughout the dog's bloodstream. If the infected dog is bitten by a mosquito, the mosquito ingests the blood and the larvae. Then Mr. Mosquito bites another dog and that dog now has heartworm larvae which will eventually mature into heartworms. This worm and all of its relatives will sooner or later block major vessels in the dog and without treatment, the dog will die.

This same dog can get a preventive medication which will kill the larvae before they can mature and cause problems. Hopefully, your veterinarian will prescribe the preventive medication as early as possible for your puppy and then check annually to ensure he is free of heartworm.

HOOKWORM

Hookworms have a life cycle of fourteen days inside a dog's intestine. In the first week the larvae develop and begin to attack to the intestinal wall and feed on the intestinal tissue. This causes inflammation, bleeding and damage to the intestine.

Treatment to eliminate hookworm is not totally effective and may have to be repeated several times. It is wise to have monthly checks and treatment until the dog is hookworm free.

ROUNDWORM

This is a very common parasite in puppies and young dogs. The eggs are ingested from heavily infected soil in small outdoor exercise areas; the eggs hatch and now the puppy has worms. If the infestation is heavy these tiny worms pass from the intestines to the lungs and liver, back to the intestines. Unfortunately, no matter how clean you may keep your puppy's environment, she may have become infested in utero if her mother had roundworms.

Just have her checked for roundworms when the hookworm check is done. Treatment is simple and effective but may need to be repeated several times.

Do not confine your puppy to concrete runs and small spaces thinking this will prevent roundworms. It may, but the prevention may cause problems far

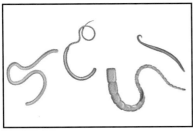

more serious—especially a lack of good muscle and tendon development as she grows. Your puppy must have adequate and good exercise if her muscles, tendons and bones are going to carry her through a good, vigorous, long life. She is not a working dog, but her build demands good muscles. Good muscle tone doesn't just happen, it must be developed. Keep the environment as clean as possible to prevent reinfestation, but not at the expense of no exercise.

Common internal parasites (l-r): roundworm, whipworm, tapeworm and hookworm.

WHIPWORM

Whipworm is similar to roundworm and causes all the problems that round- and hookworms cause, but whipworm is more difficult to detect. If the puppy continues to show symptoms of worms, it may take several stool specimens before these parasites are found and several repeated wormings before they are eliminated.

TAPEWORM

Tapeworm is common, but many veterinarians consider "tapes" relatively harmless. Tapes can be seen in dogs' stools, appearing as little white grains not unlike rice. These grains are only a section of the tape. A tape is made up of many sections, each section smaller than the one before it, with the largest section at the head. And it is true that as long as the dog retains the head of the tape, the worm is not eliminated. The tapeworm must have a host. The host is a flea that ingests the tape egg and then infects the dog. It is fairly safe to say that if your dog does not have fleas and has never had fleas, he will not have tapeworms.

GIARDIA

This parasite is actually a protozoan (single celled, usually microscopic organism) that gets into the dogs' system through infected drinking water. The primary symptom is diarrhea. Puppies are especially susceptible. These parasites are common in wild animals and if there are squirrels, raccoons, rabbits or other wild animals where puppies walk or play, there may also be Giardia. Only your veterinarian can make the diagnosis.

In summary, internal parasites may cause a problem, but with good diagnosis and proper treatment, they can be managed. Reasonable cleanliness, a good nourishing diet and exercise as the puppy grows will develop not immunity, but some control over reinfestation. Internal parasites are more of a problem for puppies than mature adults.

External Parasites

FLEAS

There is no place in the United States that is entirely free from fleas, and most of the southern states are plagued year-round. The hot, dry months usually produce the most fleas. An

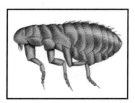

The flea is a die-hard pest.

adult flea can live for as long as two years (so when it is zero outside, be happy that the live fleas are being frozen). The adult flea can only live and reproduce where there are animals it can bite to feed off their blood. A flea bite does not only cause local itching, but may contain the larvae of the tapeworm.

If your dog has fleas, generally you will see the flea or little black leavings. Dogs with fleas will bite and scratch themselves to the point where their skin is prone to a bacterial infection. Repeated flea bites may sensitize your pet to the point that a few bites may cause a serious allergic reaction.

Not only must your dog be treated for fleas, but so must her surroundings, both inside and out. Once the dog is free of fleas, the veterinarian can give you medication that repels them. It may be necessary to have an exterminator for the house. As I have said several times, I am not a veterinarian, nor do I have a degree in the science of insects, but I must share with you my method of controlling fleas.

All of my dogs get five grains of brewers' yeast for each 10 pounds of body weight (up to six tablets) daily. The puppies are started on ½ tab daily at about 6 weeks of age (increased as the puppy grows). The pills are put on their food. My neighbors' dogs have fleas, and there are squirrels running about in the exercise areas, but our dogs do not have fleas. Mosquitoes may buzz around and bite the human population, but they light on the dogs and immediately fly away. The yeast tablets are not expensive and they are not harmful. The only disadvantage is the daily chore.

FIGHTING FLEAS

Remember, the fleas you see on your dog are only part of the problem—the smallest part! To rid your dog and home of fleas, you need to treat your dog *and* your home. Here's how:

• Identify where your pet(s) sleep. These are "hot spots."

• Clean your pets' bedding regularly by vacuuming and washing.

• Spray "hot spots" with a nontoxic, long-lasting flea larvicide.

• Treat outdoor "hot spots" with insecticide.

• Kill eggs on pets with a product containing insect growth regulators (IGRs).

• Kill fleas on pets per your veterinarian's recommendation.

TICKS

There are several kinds of ticks; the brown dog tick is quite common and can live for as long as 200 days without attaching to a dog. Once they are attached and engorged with a dog's blood, they drop off the animal and lay between 1,000 and 3,000 eggs. The eggs are usually found along baseboards, window and door cas-

ings, on the drapes and around the edges of rugs. Between feedings, the ticks usually hide in the same areas as their eggs.

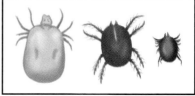

Less common are the American dog ticks, usually found out-of-

Three types of ticks (l-r): the wood tick, brown dog tick and deer tick.

doors. The American dog tick may carry Rocky Mountain Spotted Fever, tularemia and other diseases that will affect humans but not dogs. Care must be taken when removing a tick from the dog because you might be exposing yourself to any number of diseases.

Once you notice a tick, remove it at once. Swab the tick with alcohol or nail polish remover to encourage it to loosen its grip, then remove it with tweezers. Do not touch the tick with bare hands. Try to make sure the head of the tick has been removed. Wash the area with soap and dry. Check the site daily to be sure there is no infection.

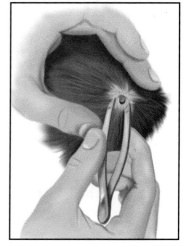

A tick infestation may call for intervention by a veterinarian. It may be

Use tweezers to remove ticks from your dog.

necessary to use chemicals and pesticides. Only your veterinarian will know what is effective and safe and the proper usage.

Spaying

When you purchased your puppy you had no intentions of breeding or raising puppies. But now, you think your Sally is such a wonderful, beautiful dog that it is wrong she will not have the opportunity to reproduce. Remember that any puppy that Sally has will only be half Sally. She cannot reproduce herself unless you resort to cloning. The best way to get another Sally is to return to Sally's parents. Even then, the many possible combinations of genes from these two is almost as great as our national debt. We can safely say there will never be another dog exactly like Sally.

But your neighbors say Sally should be bred at least once before she is spayed so she will develop and mature properly. May I remind you that very few Bulldogs whelp naturally. Cesarean sections are the rule, not the exception. There is a chance that Sally may not survive the c-section and you will have a litter of puppies to raise with no mother. Even with a mother, Bulldog puppies take your time, commitment, money and sometimes heartbreak.

If Sally has a litter, there will be little or no change in her personality. The only things that will develop are her breasts. If she has an abundance of milk and vigorous nursing puppies, her breasts will get large and floppy and will not return to the nice nipples on her tummy.

Statistics have proven that the incidence of cancer, particularly breast cancer, is reduced dramatically in spayed females. Also, a spayed female is not at risk for pyometra, a life threatening uterine infection.

Some research scientists believe that the trauma of the heat cycle is almost as great as pregnancy and puppies. In this case, it is only fair that your female be relieved of this biannual bodily function by being spayed as early as possible.

Many veterinarians advise spaying before the first heat period. Discuss the options with your vet as soon as

---

ADVANTAGES OF SPAY/NEUTER

The greatest advantage of spaying (for females) or neutering (for males) your dog is that you are guaranteed your dog will not produce puppies. There are too many puppies already available for too few homes. There are other advantages as well.

ADVANTAGES OF SPAYING

No messy heats.

No "suitors" howling at your windows or waiting in your yard.

Decreased incidences of pyometra (disease of the uterus) and breast cancer.

ADVANTAGES OF NEUTERING

Lessens male aggressive and territorial behaviors, but doesn't affect the dog's personality. Behaviors are often owner-induced, so neutering is not the only answer, but it is a good start.

Prevents the need to roam in search of bitches in season.

Decreased incidences of urogenital diseases.

possible. There is some risk in spaying, but the risk is minimal when compared to the risks involved with pregnancy and birth, as well as the risks of cancer, pyometra and unwanted pregnancy.

Neutering

Why neuter? We just won't breed him. But sooner or later, some friend will come along and convince you that it is wrong for Patrick not be allowed to sire puppies. Let me warn you of a few problems. First, Bulldogs cannot mate without help. (Almost all Bulldog breedings today are done by artificial insemination.) Secondly, once the male has been used, he will tend to forget his manners and mark his territory, including your davenport.

If Patrick has been neutered, you don't have to say "no" to your friend. It has already been said. Patrick will not be interested in the neighbors' female in season. If fact, the hormonal drive that Patrick would have and you would try to make him suppress is not present. You are both more content.

In addition, testicular cancer and other diseases of the reproductive system are prevented when you have your dog neutered.

And forget trying to make money by breeding your dog, especially your Bulldog. Artificial insemination, cesarean sections, special food, equipment, time and so on make breeding a very expensive venture. Why do

To give a pill, open the mouth wide, then drop it in the back of the throat.

I do it? Sometimes I wonder. I guess I love a challenge, and somebody has to perpetuate these wonderful dogs!

Administering Medications

Medications have become so complicated and sophisticated today that medicating your dogs yourself may just be the wrong thing to do. Few of

us can repair the systems in our cars; why do we have the audacity to believe we can practice medicine, human or animal, without preparation or education? Be sure to consult your veterinarian before giving your dog any medication.

PILLS AND CAPSULES

Using a syringe is the easiest way to administer liquid medications to your Bulldog.

Many vitamin pills now are made with a base that appeals to the dog, so he considers it a treat and eats it, but often it is not that easy. To administer pills and capsules, hide them in a piece of soft cheese, margarine, peanut butter or any other tidbit the dog especially

likes. But if he continues to spit out the pill or capsule, open his mouth and place the pill on the back of his tongue. Close his mouth, keep it closed and stroke his throat lightly or pat him on the head until he swallows. Praise, praise, praise him so the next time will be easier.

LIQUID MEDICATION

Ask your veterinarian to give you a 5 or 10 cc disposable syringe. A 5 cc syringe is easier to handle. Draw up the dose (divide if necessary) into the syringe, pull out the check pouch and slowly inject the medication, encouraging the dog to swallow. Or you can simply measure in a spoon, put medication into his mouth, close his

Squeeze eye ointment into the lower lid.

mouth and hold it closed until he swallows. Again, praise is the key word.

Do not open his mouth wide and put the medication far back into the throat, either pills or liquid. You could make him choke.

EYE MEDICATION

Do exactly as you do when putting medication in your children's eyes. Take the thumb and forefinger and hold the upper and lower lids apart and put in the ordered amount.

TOPICAL OINTMENT

If the dog can't reach the infected spot, fine. Just clean and apply the ointment. If the area is someplace the dog can reach to lick, you may have to cover it or use an Elizabethan collar. Your veterinarian will advise you on this when he prescribes the medication.

Common Problems

If you have followed the recommendations of the first part of this chapter on preventive care, your dog should have few health problems. However, should any abnormal symptoms such as vomiting, limping or diarrhea last twenty-four hours, your veterinarian should be called.

VOMITING

If it is just a one time occurrence, nothing needs to be done. However, if vomiting is persistent, contains blood, mucous or large amounts of undigested food, the veterinarian should be called.

Did the dog get into the garbage? Chew up a toy and swallow a foreign substance? Does she have a temperature? These are some of the questions you should be prepared to answer.

DIARRHEA

How long has the diarrhea lasted? If it's just a one-time problem that does not repeat in a day or two, you need not be alarmed. But if the stools are frequent for twenty-four hours or more, contain blood, mucous or undigested food, let the veterinarian make the diagnosis and prescribe the treatment. As time goes on, you will learn when to push the panic button and when to sit tight for a little while.

OVERHEATING

Bulldogs cannot tolerate heat. If they become overheated, bathe their feet and stomach with cool water or put them in a tub of cool water. If this is not possible, place baggies filled with ice under his front legs, in the groin and on his head. Wrap him in towels that have been soaked in cool water. If possible turn a fan on him. Keep him quiet. Do not give him ice chips or water unless he takes them willingly. As long as his color remains good and his breathing is regular, he probably will not require the veterinarian. But this is the decision of the veterinarian, unless you are a professional animal caretaker.

Prevention is much easier than treatment. *Never leave him in a car that is not moving,* regardless of whether windows are up or down. Never tie him to the clothesline. Exercise in the early morning or late evening. Monitor any playing of two dogs in the heat of the day.

POISONING

In every home are cleaning fluids, fingernail polish, bleach, etc. Few Bulldogs would eat or drink these things, but *no* Bulldog should have access to them. Store household necessities, fertilizers, insect sprays, etc. in cupboards and shelves. Keep the Poison Control telephone number and your veterinarian's number by your telephone.

Some of the many household substances harmful to your dog.

Call these experts for their advice. There are too many chemicals and too many complicated formula for the average person to know what action to take in an emergency. Sometimes the animal should be made

to vomit, sometimes he should have a gastric lavage (washing out of the stomach) and sometimes this action would be fatal. Only the professional can evaluate.

If your dog has eaten your prescription medication or over-the-counter pills (e.g., aspirin, Dulcolax, Tylenol, etc.), *call your veterinarian at once!* Tell him what and how much you think the dog has ingested. Some medications may depress breathing, some induce vomiting—again, only the professional person will know how to direct treatment.

Heartworm pills, flea preventive pills, in fact any medication, can cause death; prevent your dog from eating them by using good common sense in storage and housekeeping.

BURNS

Chemical—Flush with cool tap water and call the veterinarian.

Heat—If she should be burned by heat, apply ice water or fill baggies with ice cubes and lay on the burn. If the burn is extensive or third degree, only the veterinarian can direct the plan of treatment.

A first degree burn that is not extensive may only need to be kept clean and probably the only treatment needed is an over-the-counter antibiotic ointment.

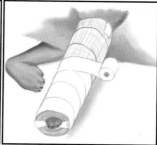

Make a temporary splint by wrapping the leg in firm casing, then bandaging it.

BROKEN BONES

Support the bone that appears to be broken and take the dog immediately to the veterinarian. X-rays are usually necessary before diagnosis can be made. What do you have about the house to use for a temporary splint? How about rolled up newspapers, or a small, thin foam rubber pillow, or a wooden spatula or a 12-inch ruler. Use your imagination and fasten the splint with adhesive tape, masking tape or strips of old sheets, and take the dog to the veterinarian for care.

EYES

If the dog has injured his eye or has something in the eye, wash it out with warm tap water if you do not have eyewash available. Do not use Boric acid or anything containing cortisone. (Prednisone and Dexamethazone are cortisone preparations and are not to be used unless ordered by the veterinarian.) Prompt diagnosis and treatment may prevent corneal damage.

BLEEDING

Apply pressure, and an ice bag if bleeding is caused by an injury. The extent of the injury and the amount of bleeding are the criteria for the need for speed and professional treatment.

Vomiting blood, blood in the urine and rectal bleeding all require diagnosis of the cause before treatment can be given. Hopefully, you have spayed your bitch, so there should not be any vaginal bleeding.

DOG BITES—ANIMAL BITES

If your dog has been bitten by who knows what, clean the wound with soap and water (preferably with

Betademic Surgical Scrub) and call your veterinarian for further orders. Check the status of her rabies vaccination. Hopefully it is current!!

BEE STINGS—SPIDER BITES

Some dogs are allergic and quick treatment is required if the dog's head, face and feet begin swelling and respiration becomes labored. During your first consultations with your veterinarian, ask him if he will

An Elizabethan collar keeps your dog from licking a fresh wound.

give you a prescription for a cortisone preparation to use in this situation or if you can give shots, he may give you Ephedrine and instruct you how and when to administer it.

In a mild allergic reaction, Benadryl can be used, can be bought over the counter and should be in your medicine cabinet. Use the straight Benadryl, not the one containing a decongestant. Benadryl does not act as quickly as Ephedrine or cortisone. Use caution if you see bees, hornets or wasps buzzing around. Try to find their nests and destroy them, but *be careful!*

CHOKING

Reach in the dog's mouth and try to pull out whatever may be choking him. Squeeze a little fresh lemon or "real" lemon juice in his mouth. Pull his tongue out to clear an airway. If whatever caused him to choke has been removed, he will probably be all right. If he continues to try to vomit, then he must go to the veterinarian for diagnosis of the cause and treatment.

Applying abdominal thrusts can save a choking dog.

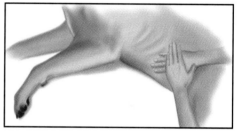

First Aid

Things to have in your medicine cabinet:

- Adhesive and masking tape

- Betademic Surgical Scrub

- Normal saline (Use as eyewash.)

- Real lemon

- Benadryl

- Kaopectate

- Peroxide (Use only on external injuries to cleanse. *Do not use in ears* unless ordered by veterinarian.)

- Thermometer

- Elastic bandages (2" and 3")

- Six packages gauze bandage (2"×3")

- Petroleum jelly

- Rubbing alcohol

WHEN TO CALL THE VET

In any emergency situation, you should call your veterinarian immediately. You can make the difference in your dog's life by staying as calm as possible when you call and by giving the doctor or the assistant as much information as possible before you leave for the clinic. That way, the vet will be able to take immediate, specific action to remedy your dog's situation.

Emergencies include acute abdominal pain, suspected poisoning, snakebite, burns, frostbite, shock, dehydration, abnormal vomiting or bleeding and deep wounds. You are the best judge of your dog's health, as you live with and observe him every day. Don't hesitate to call your veterinarian if you suspect trouble.

All of these things are what should be in a workable, useful emergency box of any family and should be checked about every three months.

Do not have Boric acid solution or powder or iodine in the emergency box. Iodine will burn sensitive tissue and Boric acid is poison!

Personally, I am not comfortable with these mini-emergency procedures. Emergencies require a cool head and knowledge. Almost as many complications develop from incorrect treatment as from lack of treatment. For instance, soap and water are the best cleansing agent. Peroxide should only be used on external wounds and never in ears. The bubbling of the peroxide may carry infection farther into the internal ear. Kaopectate is probably safe to give for a mild diarrhea (like you may have) but if blood is present, the diarrhea must be treated differently.

An injured eye may be a scratched cornea that cannot be seen without proper diagnostic equipment, and delay in diagnosis will prolong treatment. Do not use an eye ointment that contains dexamethazone unless ordered by your veterinarian.

Pesticides, herbicides, flea soaps and sprays, mange dips, etc., are so sophisticated that the more we can practice the art of prevention, the better off we and our animals will be.

One of our best "show" dog's career was ended right at its height—he trodded through puddles of a fresh rain after the grass had recently been sprayed. Within twenty-four hours, he was one big blister. His throat was so swollen that he could scarcely breathe.

After many tests, etc., he was finally diagnosed. His immune system was severely damaged and his show career over. That was a tragedy, but the *real* tragedy was the suffering of this happy, healthy dog. Keep your dogs off of sprayed grass for at least seventy-two hours. Do not use flea soaps, powder or dips without the approval of your veterinarian.

I do not want to scare you. Having a healthy dog is no more difficult than having a healthy child. Use the same common sense with your dog as you use with your child and yourself. Whenever possible, avoid prescribing medication yourself or listening to the "mini doctors" of the street. Healthy parents, immunizations, good food, exercise and reasonable cleanliness are the recipe for a healthy, happy dog and owner.

Problems Particular to Bulldogs

It may seem that man has directed the breeding of an animal with many problems. Not true. All breeds have problems they are prone to. Most of the Bulldog's problems are with reproduction and as tiny puppies. Although their life span is only about ten to fifteen years, those years are relatively healthy and happy.

HYPOTHYROIDISM

Bulldogs are subject to many of the same common ailments of other breeds. But a high percentage of Bulldogs are hypothyroids and if not treated, the complication of hypothyroidism will develop. One of the symptoms is loss of hair on the animal's sides.

Tests evaluating the thyroid function are becoming more accurate, and a tiny pill given daily will return thyroid gland function to normal.

ENTROPION

Bulldogs, because of their short faces and loose skin (wrinkles) on their faces, may have entropion eyelids. This is a condition in which the eyelashes turn in and rub against the surface of the eye. This will cause irritation and may cause blindness. The eyes are inflamed, lids swollen and there is excessive tearing. Other short-nosed breeds are subject to this same problem.

The treatment is a minor surgical procedure, or if *very* minor, your veterinarian may be able to give you

*Keep your Bulldog
at her ideal
weight—it will
increase her energy
and prevent
health problems.*

medication to instill in the eye. But this is a daily chore
and a more permanent solution is surgical intervention. Entropion is a genetic defect and dogs who are
affected should not be used for breeding.

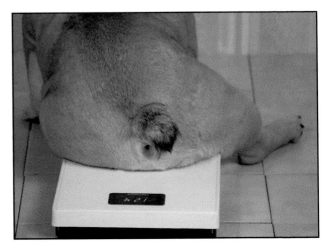

DYSPLASIA

Unfortunately Bulldogs, because of their build, may be
dysplastic. Dysplasia is a developmental disease of the
canine hip joint. It is caused by (a) increased joint lax-
ity, and (b) abnormal contours of either the ball or
socket of the hip joint.

Whatever the cause or causes of this problem, it will
eventually lead to a "remodeling" of the hip joint
and arthritis. Sometimes the pain that results can be
controlled by a cortisone preparation, but this has its
drawbacks. Excessive use of cortisone can result in
deterioration of the bone and more pain. Some
experts believe dysplasia of the hip is genetic, but it is
believed that nutritional and environmental factors
also play a roll.

ELONGATED PALATE

Loud, noisy, difficult breathing may indicate an elon-
gated palate. This can be taken care of with minor
surgery.

SWIMMING

Man and nature produced this animal with the big head and heavy shoulders and the light rear end. Because he is top heavy, many Bulldogs cannot swim. Especially he cannot swim in pools that have straight sides. He can't get out! He will drown! Sometimes he can swim in lakes and rivers.

Geriatric Care

If you get old before the dog does, he will stay by your side and care for and love you, even though you can no longer walk or play. Can you do better? The geriatric dog needs the same kind of care that geriatric people do. There is special commercial food prepared for old dogs and dogs that do not get enough exercise. Your veterinarian can direct you to the best food to get. He (the dog) will need to be groomed regularly, with particular attention to his feet and toenails. When he has his annual checkup, be sure special attention is given to his teeth.

Be sure he has fresh water at all times, and occasionally note the frequency of urination. The care of dogs is not too different from caring for a person. Puppies and babies require many of the same things, just as old dogs and old people require many of the same things. The big difference is that the dog only by his actions can tell you what hurts, while people may be inclined to verbally exaggerate their pain.

Old people and old dogs want to be loved and want attention. Old people and old dogs need exercise, and you may have to insist they get it. Sometimes you may need to entice them to eat. But they will still enjoy being brushed and groomed, still enjoy being the center of attention and not shoved back in some dark room. Just don't expect them to romp as vigorously or walk as fast or play as hard; their bodies are old even though their spirits are young.

A lot of prevention, a little common sense and love and your dog and you will have a wonderful life together.

Euthanasia

A part of the care you owe your dog is relief from pain when life is no longer life. Memories are wonderful. All the beautiful days and fun times are remembered, the problems forgotten!

I would like to share with you how I have learned to bring some kind of closure to this dog's life and the lives of my human friends as the need arises.

I write them a letter remembering the years we had together, good things, bad things, everything and then I thank my God for the wonderful privilege of lives shared.

So be it!

My Dog
Who knows my every step,
my nature and its mood?
Who forgets my anger,
And helps me not waste food?

Who coaxes me to play,
And sits at my command?
Who shares my heavy load
With brown eyes that understand?

Who guards my humble home,
And to my chair lays claim?
Who loves without question,
And tracks mud in with the rain?
<u>MY BULLDOG, MY FRIEND</u>
<u>GOD BLESS HIM</u>

Your Happy, Healthy Pet

Your Dog's Name _____

Name on Your Dog's Pedigree (if your dog has one) _____

_____

Where Your Dog Came From _____

_____

Your Dog's Birthday _____

Your Dog's Veterinarian

    Name _____

    Address _____

    Phone Number_____

    Emergency Number_____

Your Dog's Health

    Vaccines

    type _____ date given _____

    type _____ date given _____

    type _____ date given _____

    type _____ date given _____

    Heartworm

    date tested _____ type used_____ start date _____

Your Dog's License Number_____

Groomer's Name and Number _____

Dogsitter/Walker's Name and Number_____

Awards Your Dog Has Won

    Award _____ date earned _____

    Award _____ date earned _____

part three

Enjoying
your
Dog

chapter 8

Basic
Training

by Ian Dunbar, Ph.D., MRCVS

Training is the jewel in the crown—the most important aspect of doggy husbandry. There is no more important variable influencing dog behavior and temperament than the dog's education: A well-trained, well-behaved and good-natured puppydog is always a joy to live with, but an untrained and uncivilized dog can be a perpetual nightmare. Moreover, deny the dog an education and it will not have the opportunity to fulfill its own canine potential; neither will it have the ability to communicate effectively with its human companions.

Luckily, modern psychological training methods are easy, efficient and effective and, above all, considerably dog-friendly and user-friendly. Doggy education is as simple as it is enjoyable. But before

98

you can have a good time play-training with your new dog, you have to learn what to do and how to do it. There is no bigger variable influencing the success of dog training than the *owner's* experience and expertise. *Before you embark on the dog's education, you must first educate yourself.*

Basic Training for Owners

Ideally, basic owner training should begin well *before* you select your dog. Find out all you can about your chosen breed first, then master rudimentary training and handling skills. If you already have your puppy/dog, owner training is a dire emergency—the clock is running! Especially for puppies, the first few weeks at home are the most important and influential days in the dog's life. Indeed, the cause of most adolescent and adult problems may be traced back to the initial days the pup explores his new home. This is the time to establish the *status quo*—to teach the puppy/dog how you would like him to behave and so prevent otherwise quite predictable problems.

In addition to consulting breeders and breed books such as this one (which understandably have a positive breed bias), seek out as many pet owners with your breed you can find. Good points are obvious. What you want to find out are the breed-specific *problems,* so you can nip them in the bud. In particular, you should talk to owners with *adolescent* dogs and make a list of all anticipated problems. Most important, *test drive* at least half a dozen adolescent and adult dogs of your breed yourself. An eight-week-old puppy is deceptively easy to handle, but she will acquire adult size, speed and strength in just four months, so you should learn now what to prepare for.

Puppy and pet dog training classes offer a convenient venue to locate pet owners and observe dogs in action. For a list of suitable trainers in your area, contact the Association of Pet Dog Trainers (see Chapter 13). You may also begin your basic owner training by observing other owners in class. Watch as many classes and test drive as many dogs as possible. Select an upbeat, dog-friendly, people-friendly, fun-and-games, puppydog pet training class to learn the ropes. Also, watch training videos and read training books (see Chapter 12). You must find out what to do and how to do it *before* you have to do it.

Principles of Training

Most people think training comprises teaching the dog to do things such as sit, speak and roll over, but even a four-week-old pup knows how to do these things already. Instead, the first step in training involves teaching the dog human words for each dog behavior and activity and for each aspect of the dog's environment. That way you, the owner, can more easily participate in the dog's domestic education by directing him to perform specific actions appropriately, that is, at the right time, in the right place, and so on. Training opens communication channels, enabling an educated dog to at least understand the owner's requests.

In addition to teaching a dog *what* we want her to do, it is also necessary to teach her *why* she should do what we ask. Indeed, 95 percent of training revolves around motivating the dog *to want to do* what we want. Dogs often understand what their owners want; they just don't see the point of doing it—especially when the owner's repetitively boring and seemingly senseless instructions are totally at odds with much more pressing and exciting doggy distractions. It is not so much the dog who is being stubborn or dominant; rather, it is the owner who has failed to acknowledge the dog's needs and feelings and to approach training from the dog's point of view.

The Meaning of Instructions

The secret to successful training is learning how to use training lures to predict or prompt specific behaviors—to coax the dog to do what you want *when* you want. Any highly valued object (such as a treat or toy) may be used as a lure, which the dog will follow with his eyes and nose. Moving the lure in specific ways entices the dog to move his nose, head and entire body in specific ways. In fact, by learning the art of manipulating various lures, it is possible to teach the dog to assume virtually any body position and perform any action. Once you have control over the expression of the dog's behaviors and can elicit any body position or behavior at will, you can easily teach the dog to perform on request.

Tell your dog what you want him to do, use a lure to entice him to respond correctly, then profusely praise

Teach your dog words for each activity he needs to know, like down.

and maybe reward him once he performs the desired action. For example, verbally request "Fido, sit!" while you move a squeaky toy upwards and backwards over the dog's muzzle (lure-movement and hand signal), smile knowingly as he looks up (to follow the lure) and sits down (as a result of canine anatomical engineering), then praise him to distraction ("Gooood Fido!"). Squeak the toy, offer a training treat and give your dog and yourself a pat on the back.

Being able to elicit desired responses over and over enables the owner to reward the dog over and over. Consequently, the dog begins to think training is fun. For example, the more the dog is rewarded for sitting, the more she enjoys sitting. Eventually the dog comes to realize that, whereas most sitting is appreciated, sitting immediately upon request usually prompts especially enthusiastic praise and a slew of high-level rewards. The dog begins to sit on cue much of the time, showing that she is starting to grasp the meaning of the owner's verbal request and hand signal.

Why Comply?

Most dogs enjoy initial lure/reward training and are only too happy to comply with their owners' wishes. Unfortunately, repetitive drilling without appreciative feedback tends to diminish the dog's enthusiasm until he eventually fails to see the point of complying anymore. Moreover, as the dog approaches adolescence he becomes more easily distracted as he develops other interests. Lengthy sessions with repetitive exercises tend to bore and demotivate both parties. If it's not fun, the owner doesn't do it and neither does the dog.

Integrate training into your dog's life: The greater number of training sessions each day and the *shorter* they are, the more willingly compliant your dog will become. Make sure to have a short (just a few seconds) training interlude before every enjoyable canine activity. For example, ask your dog to sit to greet people, to sit before you throw his Frisbee, and to sit for his supper. Really, sitting is no different from a canine "please." Also, include numerous short training interludes during every enjoyable canine pastime, for example, when playing with the dog or when he is running in the park. In this fashion, doggy distractions may be effectively converted into rewards for training. Just as all games have rules, fun becomes training . . . and training becomes fun.

Eventually, rewards actually become unnecessary to continue motivating your dog. If trained with consideration and kindness, performing the desired behaviors will become self-rewarding and, in a sense, your dog will motivate himself. Just as it is not necessary to reward a human companion during an enjoyable walk in the park, or following a game of tennis, it is hardly necessary to reward our best friend—the dog—for walking by our side or while playing fetch. Human company during enjoyable activities is reward enough for most dogs.

Even though your dog has become self-motivating, it's still good to praise and pet him a lot and offer rewards once in a while, especially for a good job well done. And if for no other reason, praising and rewarding others is good for the human heart.

To train your dog, you need gentle hands, a loving heart and a good attitude.

Punishment

Without a doubt, lure/reward training is by far the best way to teach: Entice your dog to do what you want and then reward him for doing so. Unfortunately, a human shortcoming is to take the good for granted and to moan and groan at the bad. Specifically, the dog's many good behaviors are ignored while the owner focuses on punishing the dog for making mistakes. In extreme cases, instruction is *limited* to punishing mistakes made by a trainee dog, child, employee or husband, even though it has been proven punishment training is notoriously inefficient and ineffective and is decidedly unfriendly and combative. It teaches the dog that training is a drag, almost as quickly as it teaches the dog to dislike his trainer. Why treat our best friends like our worst enemies?

Punishment training is also much more laborious and time consuming. Whereas it takes only a finite amount of time to teach a dog what to chew, for example, it takes much, much longer to punish the dog for each and every mistake. Remember, *there is only one right way!* So why not teach that right way from the outset?!

To make matters worse, punishment training causes severe lapses in the dog's reliability. Since it is obviously impossible to punish the dog each and every time she misbehaves, the dog quickly learns to distinguish between those times when she must comply (so as to avoid impending punishment) and those times when she need not comply, because punishment is impossible. Such times include when the dog is off leash and only six feet away, when the owner is otherwise engaged (talking to a friend, watching television, taking a shower, tending to the baby or chatting on the telephone), or when the dog is left at home alone.

Instances of misbehavior will be numerous when the owner is away, because even when the dog complied in the owner's looming presence, he did so unwillingly. The dog was forced to act against his will, rather than moulding his will to want to please. Hence, when the owner is absent, not only does the dog know he need not comply, he simply does not want to. Again, the trainee is not a stubborn vindictive beast, but rather the trainer has failed to teach.

Punishment training invariably creates unpredictable Jekyll and Hyde behavior.

Trainer's Tools

Many training books extol the virtues of a vast array of training paraphernalia and electronic and metallic gizmos, most of which are designed for canine restraint, correction and punishment, rather than for actual facilitation of doggy education. In reality, most effective training tools are not found in stores; they come from within ourselves. In addition to a willing dog, all you really need is a functional human brain, gentle hands, a loving heart and a good attitude.

In terms of equipment, all dogs do require a quality buckle collar to sport dog tags and to attach the leash (for safety and to comply with local leash laws). Hollow chewtoys (like Kongs or sterilized longbones) and a dog bed or collapsible crate are a must for housetraining. Three additional tools are required:

1. specific lures (training treats and toys) to predict and prompt specific desired behaviors;

2. rewards (praise, affection, training treats and toys) to reinforce for the dog what a lot of fun it all is; and

3. knowledge—how to convert the dog's favorite activities and games (potential distractions to training) into "life-rewards," which may be employed to facilitate training.

The most powerful of these is *knowledge*. Education is the key! Watch training classes, participate in training classes, watch videos, read books, enjoy playtraining with your dog, and then your dog will say "Please," and your dog will say "Thank you!"

Housetraining

If dogs were left to their own devices, certainly they would chew, dig and bark for entertainment and then no doubt highlight a few areas of their living space with sprinkles of urine, in much the same way we decorate by hanging pictures. Consequently, when we ask a dog to live with us, we must teach him *where* he may dig and perform his toilet duties, *what* he may chew and *when* he may bark. After all, when left at home alone for many hours, we cannot expect the dog to amuse himself by completing crosswords or watching the soaps on TV!

Also, it would be decidedly unfair to keep the house rules a secret from the dog, and then get angry and punish the poor critter for inevitably transgressing rules he did not even know existed. Remember, without adequate education and guidance, the dog will be forced to establish his own rules—doggy rules—that most probably will be at odds with the owner's view of domestic living.

Since most problems develop during the first few days the dog is at home, prospective dog owners must be certain they are quite clear about the principles of housetraining *before* they get a dog. Early misbehaviors quickly become established as the status quo—

becoming firmly entrenched as hard-to-break bad habits, which set the precedent for years to come. Make sure to teach your dog good habits right from the start. Good habits are just as hard to break as bad ones!

Ideally, when a new dog comes home, try to arrange for someone to be present for as much as possible during the first few days (for adult dogs) or weeks for puppies. With only a little forethought, it is surprisingly easy to find a puppy sitter, such as a retired person, who would be willing to eat from your refrigerator and watch your television while keeping an eye on the newcomer to encourage the dog to play with chewtoys and to ensure he goes outside on a regular basis.

POTTY TRAINING

To teach the dog where to relieve himself:

1. never let him make a single mistake;

2. let him know where you want him to go; and

3. handsomely reward him for doing so: "GOOOOOOOD DOG!!!" liver treat, liver treat, liver treat!

PREVENTING MISTAKES

A single mistake is a training disaster, since it heralds many more in future weeks. And each time the dog soils the house, this further reinforces the dog's unfortunate preference for an indoor, carpeted toilet. *Do not let an unhousetrained dog have full run of the house if you are away from home or cannot pay full attention.* Instead, confine the dog to an area where elimination is appropriate, such as an outdoor run or, better still, a small, comfortable indoor kennel with access to an outdoor run. When confined in this manner, most dogs will naturally housetrain themselves.

If that's not possible, confine the dog to an area, such as a utility room, kitchen, basement or garage, where elimination may not be desired in the long run but as an interim measure it is certainly preferable to doing it all around the house. Use newspaper to cover the floor of the dog's day room. The newspaper may be used to soak up the urine and to wrap up and dispose of the feces. Once your dog develops a preferred spot for eliminating, it is only necessary to cover that part of the floor with newspaper. The smaller papered area may then be moved (only a little each day) towards the door to the outside. Thus the dog will develop the tendency to go to the door when he needs to relieve himself.

Never confine an unhousetrained dog to a crate for long periods. Doing so would force the dog to soil the crate and ruin its usefulness as an aid for housetraining (see the following discussion).

The first few weeks at home are the most important and influential in your dog's life.

TEACHING WHERE

In order to teach your dog where you would like her to do her business, you have to be there to direct the proceedings—an obvious, yet often neglected, fact of life. In order to be there to teach the dog *where* to go, you need to know *when* she needs to go. Indeed, the success of housetraining depends on the owner's ability to predict these times. Certainly, a regular feeding schedule will facilitate prediction somewhat, but there is

nothing like "loading the deck" and influencing the timing of the outcome yourself!

Whenever you are at home, make sure the dog is under constant supervision and/or confined to a small area. If already well trained, simply instruct the dog to lie down in his bed or basket. Alternatively, confine the dog to a crate (doggy den) or tie-down (a short, 18-inch lead that can be clipped to an eye hook in the baseboard). Short-term close confinement strongly inhibits urination and defecation, since the dog does not want to soil his sleeping area. Thus, when you release the puppydog each hour, he will definitely need to urinate immediately and defecate every third or fourth hour. Keep the dog confined to his doggy den and take him to his intended toilet area each hour, every hour, and on the hour.

When taking your dog outside, instruct him to sit quietly before opening the door—he will soon learn to sit by the door when he needs to go out!

TEACHING WHY

Being able to predict when the dog needs to go enables the owner to be on the spot to praise and reward the dog. Each hour, hurry the dog to the intended toilet area in the yard, issue the appropriate instruction ("Go pee!" or "Go poop!"), then give the dog three to four minutes to produce. Praise and offer a couple of training treats when successful. The treats are important because many people fail to praise their dogs with feeling . . . and housetraining is hardly the time for understatement. So either loosen up and enthusiastically praise that dog: "Wuzzzer-wuzzer-wuzzer, hoooser good wuffer den? Hoooo went pee for Daddy?" Or say "Good dog!" as best you can and offer the treats for effect.

Following elimination is an ideal time for a spot of playtraining in the yard or house. Also, an empty dog may be allowed greater freedom around the house for the next half hour or so, just as long as you keep an eye out to make sure he does not get into other kinds of mischief. If you are preoccupied and cannot pay full attention, confine the dog to his doggy den once more to enjoy a peaceful snooze or to play with his many chewtoys.

If your dog does not eliminate within the allotted time outside—no biggie! Back to his doggy den, and then try again after another hour.

As I own large dogs, I always feel more relaxed walking an empty dog, knowing that I will not need to finish our stroll weighted down with bags of feces! Beware of falling into the trap of walking the dog to get it to eliminate. The good ol' dog walk is such an enormous highlight in the dog's life that it represents the single biggest potential reward in domestic dogdom. However, when in a hurry, or during inclement weather, many owners abruptly terminate the walk the moment the dog has done its business. This, in effect, severely punishes the dog for doing the right thing, in the right place at the right time. Consequently, many dogs become strongly inhibited from eliminating outdoors because they know it will signal an abrupt end to an otherwise thoroughly enjoyable walk.

Instead, instruct the dog to relieve himself in the yard prior to going for a walk. If you follow the above instructions, most dogs soon learn to eliminate on cue. As soon as the dog eliminates, praise (and offer a treat or two)—"Good dog! Let's go walkies!" Use the walk as a reward for eliminating in the yard. If the dog does not go, put him back in his doggy den and think about a walk later on. You will find with a "No feces–no walk" policy, your dog will become one of the fastest defecators in the business.

If you do not have a back yard, instruct the dog to eliminate right outside your front door prior to the walk. Not only will this facilitate clean up and disposal of the feces in your own trash can but, also, the walk may again be used as a colossal reward.

CHEWING AND BARKING

Short-term close confinement also teaches the dog that occasional quiet moments are a reality of domestic living. Your puppydog is extremely impressionable during his first few weeks at home. Regular confinement at this time soon exerts a calming influence over the dog's personality. Remember, once the dog is housetrained and calmer, there will be a whole lifetime ahead for the dog to enjoy full run of the house and garden. On the other hand, by letting the newcomer have unrestricted access to the entire household and allowing him to run willy-nilly, he will most certainly develop a bunch of behavior problems in short order, no doubt necessitating confinement later in life. It would not be fair to remedially restrain and confine a dog you have trained, through neglect, to run free.

When confining the dog, make sure he always has an impressive array of suitable chewtoys. Kongs and sterilized longbones (both readily available from pet stores) make the best chewtoys, since they are hollow and may be stuffed with treats to heighten the dog's interest. For example, by stuffing the little hole at the top of a Kong with a small piece of freeze-dried liver, the dog will not want to leave it alone.

Remember, treats do not have to be junk food and they certainly should not represent extra calories. Rather, treats should be part of each dog's regular daily diet:

Make sure your puppy has suitable chewtoys.

Some food may be served in the dog's bowl for breakfast and dinner, some food may be used as training treats, and some food may be used for stuffing chewtoys. I regularly stuff my dogs' many Kongs with different shaped biscuits and kibble. The kibble seems to fall out fairly easily, as do the oval-shaped biscuits, thus rewarding the dog instantaneously for checking out the chewtoys. The bone-shaped biscuits fall out after a while, rewarding the dog for worrying at the chewtoy. But the triangular biscuits never come out. They remain inside the Kong as lures, maintaining the dog's fascination with its chewtoy. To further focus the dog's interest, I always make sure to flavor the triangular biscuits by rubbing them with a little cheese or freeze-dried liver.

If stuffed chewtoys are reserved especially for times the dog is confined, the puppydog will soon learn to enjoy quiet moments in her doggy den and she will quickly develop a chewtoy habit—a good habit! This is a simple *passive training* process; all the owner has to do is set up the situation and the dog all but trains herself—easy and effective. Even when the dog is given run of the house, her first inclination will be to indulge her rewarding chewtoy habit rather than destroying less-attractive household articles, such as curtains, carpets, chairs and compact disks. Similarly, a chewtoy chewer will be less inclined to scratch and chew herself excessively. Also, if the dog busies herself as a recreational chewer, she will be less inclined to develop into a recreational barker or digger when left at home alone.

Stuff a number of chewtoys whenever the dog is left confined and remove the extra-special-tasting treats when you return. Your dog will now amuse himself with his chewtoys before falling asleep and then resume playing with his chewtoys when he expects you to return. Since most owner-absent misbehavior happens right after you leave and right before your expected return, your puppydog will now be conveniently preoccupied with his chewtoys at these times.

To teach come, call your dog, open your arms as a welcoming signal, wave a toy or a treat and praise for every step in your direction.

Come and Sit

Most puppies will happily approach virtually anyone, whether called or not; that is, until they collide with adolescence and develop other more important doggy interests, such as sniffing a multiplicity of exquisite odors on the grass. Your mission, Mr. and/or Ms. Owner, is to teach and reward the pup for coming reliably, willingly and happily when called—and you have just three months to get it done. Unless adequately reinforced, your puppy's tendency to approach people will self-destruct by adolescence.

Call your dog ("Fido, come!"), open your arms (and maybe squat down) as a welcoming signal, waggle a treat or toy as a lure, and reward the puppydog when he comes running. Do not wait to praise the dog until he reaches you—he may come 95 percent of the way and then run off after some distraction. Instead, praise the dog's *first* step towards you and continue praising enthusiastically for *every* step he takes in your direction.

When the rapidly approaching puppy dog is three lengths away from impact, instruct him to sit ("Fido, sit!") and hold the lure in front of you in an outstretched hand to prevent him from hitting you mid-chest and knocking you flat on your back! As Fido decelerates to nose the lure, move the treat upwards and backwards just over his muzzle with an upwards motion of your extended arm (palm-upwards). As the dog looks up to follow the lure, he will sit down (if he jumps up, you are holding the lure too high). Praise the dog for sitting. Move backwards and call him again. Repeat this many times over, always praising when Fido comes and sits; on occasion, reward him.

For the first couple of trials, use a training treat both as a lure to entice the dog to come and sit and as a reward for doing so. Thereafter, try to use different items as lures and rewards. For example, lure the dog with a Kong or Frisbee but reward her with a food treat. Or lure the dog with a food treat but pat her and throw a tennis ball as a reward. After just a few repetitions, dispense with the lures and rewards; the dog will begin to respond willingly to your verbal requests and hand signals just for the prospect of praise from your heart and affection from your hands.

Instruct every family member, friend and visitor how to get the dog to come and sit. Invite people over for a series of pooch parties; do not keep the pup a secret—let other people enjoy this puppy, and let the pup enjoy other people. Puppydog parties are not only fun, they easily attract a lot of people to help *you* train *your* dog. Unless you teach your dog *how* to meet people, that is, to sit for greetings, no doubt the dog will resort to jumping up. Then you and the visitors will get annoyed, and the dog will be punished. This is not fair. *Send out those invitations for puppy parties and teach your dog to be mannerly and socially acceptable.*

Even though your dog quickly masters obedient recalls in the house, his reliability may falter when playing in the back yard or local park. Ironically, it is *the owner* who has unintentionally trained the dog *not* to respond in these instances. By allowing the dog to play and run around and otherwise have a good time, but then to call the dog to put him on leash to take him home, the dog quickly learns playing is fun but training is a drag. Thus, playing in the park becomes a severe distraction, which works against training. Bad news!

Instead, whether playing with the dog off leash or on leash, request him to come at frequent intervals—say, every minute or so. On most occasions, praise and pet the dog for a few seconds while he is sitting, then tell him to go play again. For especially fast recalls, offer a couple of training treats and take the time to praise and pet the dog enthusiastically before releasing him. The dog will learn that coming when called is not necessarily the end of the play session, and neither is it the end of the world; rather, it signals an enjoyable, quality time-out with the owner before resuming play once more. In fact, playing in the park now becomes a very effective life-reward, which works to facilitate training by reinforcing each obedient and timely recall. Good news!

Sit, Down, Stand and Rollover

Teaching the dog a variety of body positions is easy for owner and dog, impressive for spectators and extremely useful for all. Using lure-reward techniques, it is possible to train several positions at once to verbal commands or hand signals (which impress the socks off onlookers).

Sit and *down*—the two control commands—prevent or resolve nearly a hundred behavior problems. For example, if the dog happily and obediently sits or lies down when requested, he cannot jump on visitors, dash out the front door, run around and chase its tail, pester other dogs, harass cats or annoy family, friends or strangers. Additionally, "sit" or "down" are better emergency commands for off-leash control.

It is easier to teach and maintain a reliable sit than maintain a reliable recall. *Sit* is the purest and simplest of commands—either the dog is sitting or he is not. If there is any change of circumstances or potential danger in the park, for example, simply instruct the dog to sit. If he sits, you have a number of options: allow the dog to resume playing when he is safe; walk up and put the dog on leash, or call the dog. The dog will be much more likely to come when called if he has already acknowledged his compliance by sitting. If the dog does not sit in the park—train him to!

Stand and *rollover-stay* are the two positions for examining the dog. Your veterinarian will love you to distraction if you take a little time to teach the dog to stand still and roll over and play possum. Also, your vet bills will be smaller. The rollover-stay is an especially useful command and is really just a variation of the down-stay: whereas the dog lies prone in the traditional down, she lies supine in the rollover-stay.

As with teaching come and sit, the training techniques to teach the dog to assume all other body positions on cue are user-friendly and dog-friendly. Simply give the appropriate request, lure the dog into the desired body position using a training treat or toy and then *praise* (and maybe reward) the dog as soon as he complies. Try not to touch the dog to get him to respond. If you teach the dog by guiding him into position, the dog will quickly learn that rump-pressure means sit, for example, but as yet you still have no control over your dog if he is just six feet away. It will still be necessary to teach the dog to sit on request. So do not make training a time-consuming two-step process; instead, teach the dog to sit to a verbal request or hand signal from the outset. Once the dog sits willingly when requested, by all means use your hands to pet the dog when he does so.

To teach *down* when the dog is already sitting, say "Fido, down!," hold the lure in one hand (palm down) and lower that hand to the floor between the dog's forepaws. As the dog lowers his head to follow the lure, slowly move the lure away from the dog just a fraction (in front of his paws). The dog will lie down as he stretches his nose forward to follow the lure. Praise the dog when he does so. If the dog stands up, you pulled the lure away too far and too quickly.

When teaching the dog to lie down from the standing position, say "down" and lower the lure to the floor as before. Once the dog has lowered his forequarters and assumed a play bow, gently and slowly move the lure *towards* the dog between his forelegs. Praise the dog as soon as his rear end plops down.

After just a couple of trials it will be possible to alternate sits and downs and have the dog energetically perform doggy push-ups. Praise the dog a lot, and after half a dozen or so push-ups reward the dog with a training treat or toy. You will notice the more energetically you move your arm—upwards (palm up) to get the dog to sit, and downwards (palm down) to get the dog to lie down—the more energetically the dog responds to your requests. Now try training the dog in silence and you will notice he has also learned to respond to hand signals. Yeah! Not too shabby for the first session.

To teach *stand* from the sitting position, say "Fido, stand," slowly move the lure half a dog-length away from the dog's nose, keeping it at nose level, and praise the dog as he stands to follow the lure. As soon

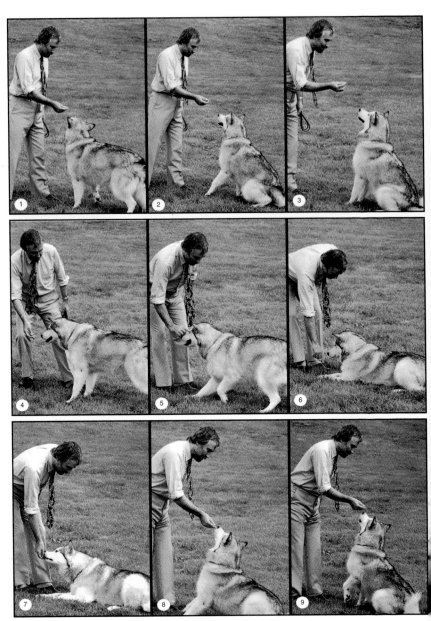

Using a food lure to teach sit, down and stand. 1) "Phoenix, Sit." 2) Hand palm upwards, move lure up and back over dog's muzzle. 3) "Good sit, Phoenix!" 4) "Phoenix, down." 5) Hand palm downwards, move lure down to lie between dog's forepaws. 6) "Phoenix, off. Good down, Phoenix!" 7) "Phoenix, sit!" 8) Palm upwards, move lure up and back, keeping it close to dog's muzzle. 9) "Good sit, Phoenix!"

10) *"Phoenix, stand!"* 11) *Move lure away from dog at nose height, then lower it a tad.* 12) *"Phoenix, off! Good stand, Phoenix!"* 13) *"Phoenix, down!"* 14) *Hand palm downwards, move lure down to lie between dog's forepaws.* 15) *"Phoenix, off! Good down-stay, Phoenix!"* 16) *"Phoenix, stand!"* 17) *Move lure away from dog's muzzle up to nose height.* 18) *"Phoenix, off! Good stand-stay, Phoenix. Now we'll make the vet and groomer happy!"*

as the dog stands, lower the lure to just beneath the dog's chin to entice him to look down; otherwise he will stand and then sit immediately. To prompt the dog to stand from the down position, move the lure half a dog-length upwards and away from the dog, holding the lure at standing nose height from the floor.

Teaching *rollover* is best started from the down position, with the dog lying on one side, or at least with both hind legs stretched out on the same side. Say "Fido, bang!" and move the lure backwards and alongside the dog's muzzle to its elbow (on the side of its outstretched hind legs). Once the dog looks to the side and backwards, very slowly move the lure upwards to the dog's shoulder and backbone. Tickling the dog in the goolies (groin area) often invokes a reflex-raising of the hind leg as an appeasement gesture, which facilitates the tendency to roll over. If you move the lure too quickly and the dog jumps into the standing position, have patience and start again. As soon as the dog rolls onto its back, keep the lure stationary and mesmerize the dog with a relaxing tummy rub.

To teach *rollover-stay* when the dog is standing or moving, say "Fido, bang!" and give the appropriate hand signal (with index finger pointed and thumb cocked in true Sam Spade fashion), then in one fluid movement lure him to first lie down and then rollover-stay as above.

Teaching the dog to *stay* in each of the above four positions becomes a piece of cake after first teaching the dog not to worry at the toy or treat training lure. This is best accomplished by hand feeding dinner kibble. Hold a piece of kibble firmly in your hand and softly instruct "Off!" Ignore any licking and slobbering *for however long the dog worries at the treat*, but say "Take it!" and offer the kibble *the instant* the dog breaks contact with his muzzle. Repeat this a few times, and then up the ante and insist the dog remove his muzzle for one whole second before offering the kibble. Then progressively refine your criteria and have the dog not touch your hand (or treat) for longer and longer periods on each trial, such as for two seconds, four seconds, then six, ten, fifteen, twenty, thirty seconds and so on. The dog soon learns: (1) worrying at the treat never gets results, whereas (2) noncontact is often rewarded after a variable time lapse.

Teaching *"Off!"* has many useful applications in its own right. Additionally, instructing the dog not to touch a training lure often produces spontaneous and magical stays. Request the dog to stand-stay, for example, and not to touch the lure. At first set your sights on a short two-second stay before rewarding the dog. (Remember, every long journey begins with a single step.) However, on subsequent trials, gradually and progressively increase the length of stay required to receive a reward. In no time at all your dog will stand calmly for a minute or so.

Relevancy Training

Once you have taught the dog what you expect her to do when requested to come, sit, lie down, stand, rollover and stay, the time is right to teach the dog *why* she should comply with your wishes. The secret is to have many (*many*) extremely short training interludes (two to five seconds each) at numerous (*numerous*) times during the course of the dog's day. Especially work with the dog immediately *before* the dog's good times and *during* the dog's good times. For example, ask your dog to sit and/or lie down each time before opening doors, serving meals, offering treats and tummy rubs; ask the dog to perform a few controlled doggy push-ups before letting her off-leash or throwing a tennis ball; and perhaps request the dog to sit-down-sit-stand-down-stand-rollover before inviting her to cuddle on the couch.

Similarly, request the dog to sit many times during play or on walks, and in no time at all the dog will be only too pleased to follow your instructions because he has learned that a compliant response heralds all sorts of goodies. Basically all you are trying to teach the dog is how to say please: "Please throw the tennis ball. Please may I snuggle on the couch."

Remember, whereas it is important to keep training interludes short, it is equally important to have many short sessions each and every day. The shortest (and most useful) session comprises asking the dog to sit and then go play during a play session. When trained this way, your dog will soon associate training with good times. In fact, the dog may be unable to distinguish between training and good times and, indeed, there should be no distinction. The warped concept that training involves forcing the dog to comply and/or dominating his will is totally at odds with the picture of a truly well-trained dog. In reality, enjoying a game of training with a dog is no different from enjoying a game of backgammon or tennis with a friend; and walking with a dog should be no different from strolling with buddies on the golf course.

Walk by Your Side

Many people attempt to teach a dog to heel by putting him on a leash and physically correcting the dog when he makes mistakes. There are a number of things seriously wrong with this approach, the first being that most people do not want precision heeling; rather, they simply want the dog to follow or walk by their side. Second, when physically restrained during "training," even though the dog may grudgingly mope by your side when "handcuffed" on leash, let's see what happens when he is off leash. History! The dog is in the next county because he never enjoyed walking with you on leash and you have no control over him off leash. So let's just teach the dog off leash from the outset to *want* to walk with us. Third, if the dog has not been trained to heel, it is a trifle hasty to think about punishing the poor dog for making mistakes and breaking heeling rules he didn't even know existed. This is simply not fair! Surely, if the dog had been adequately taught how to heel, he would seldom make mistakes and hence there would be no need to correct the dog. Remember, each mistake and each correction (punishment) advertise the trainer's inadequacy, not the dog's. The dog is not stubborn, he is not stupid and he is not bad. Even if he were, he would still require training, so let's train him properly.

Let's teach the dog to *enjoy* following us and to *want* to walk by our side offleash. Then it will be easier to teach high-precision off-leash heeling patterns if desired. After attaching the leash for safety on outdoor walks, but before going anywhere, it is necessary to teach the dog specifically not to pull. Now it will be much easier to teach on-leash walking and heeling because the dog already wants to walk with you, he is familiar with the desired walking and heeling positions and he knows not to pull.

FOLLOWING

Start by training your dog to follow you. Many puppies will follow if you simply walk away from them and maybe click your fingers or chuckle. Adult dogs may require additional enticement to stimulate them to follow, such as a training lure or, at the very least, a lively trainer. To teach the dog to follow: (1) keep walking and (2) walk away from the dog. If the dog attempts to lead or lag, change pace; slow down if the dog forges too far ahead, but speed up if he lags too far behind. Say "Steady!" or "Easy!" each time before you slow down and "Quickly!" or "Hustle!" each time before you speed up, and the dog will learn to change pace on cue. If the dog lags or leads too far, or if he wanders right or left, simply walk quickly in the opposite direction and maybe even run away from the dog and hide.

Practicing is a lot of fun; you can set up a course in your home, yard or park to do this. Indoors, entice the dog to follow upstairs, into a bedroom, into the bathroom, downstairs, around the living room couch, zigzagging between dining room chairs and into the kitchen for dinner. Outdoors, get the dog to follow around park benches, trees, shrubs and along walkways and lines in the grass. (For safety outdoors, it is advisable to attach a long line on the dog, but never exert corrective tension on the line.)

Remember, following has a lot to do with attitude—*your* attitude! Most probably your dog will *not* want to follow Mr. Grumpy Troll with the personality of wilted lettuce. Lighten up—walk with a jaunty step, whistle a happy tune, sing, skip and tell jokes to your dog and he will be right there by your side.

BY YOUR SIDE

It is smart to train the dog to walk close on one side or the other—either side will do, your choice. When walking, jogging or cycling, it is generally bad news to have the dog suddenly cut in front of you. In fact, I train my dogs to walk "By my side" and "Other side"—both very useful instructions. It is possible to position the dog fairly accurately by looking to the appropriate side and clicking your fingers or slapping your thigh on that side. A precise positioning may be attained by holding a training lure, such as a chewtoy, tennis ball, or food treat. Stop and stand still several times throughout the walk, just as you would when window shopping or meeting a friend. Use the lure to make sure the dog slows down and stays close whenever you stop.

When teaching the dog to heel, we generally want her to sit in heel position when we stop. Teach heel

Using a toy to teach sit-heel-sit sequences: 1) "Phoenix, heel!" Standing still, move lure up and back over dog's muzzle.... 2) To position dog sitting in heel position on your left side. 3) "Phoenix, heel!" wagging lure in left hand. Change lure to right hand in preparation for sit signal.

122

position at the standstill and the dog will learn that the default heel position is sitting by your side (left or right—your choice, unless you wish to compete in obedience trials, in which case the dog must heel on the left).

Several times a day, stand up and call your dog to come and sit in heel position—"Fido, heel!" For example, instruct the dog to come to heel each time there are commercials on TV, or each time you turn a page of a novel, and the dog will get it in a single evening.

Practice straight-line heeling and turns separately. With the dog sitting at heel, teach him to turn in place. After each quarter-turn, half-turn or full turn in place, lure the dog to sit at heel. Now it's time for short straight-line heeling sequences, no more than a few steps at a time. Always think of heeling in terms of Sit-Heel-Sit sequences—start and end with the dog in position and do your best to keep him there when moving. Progressively increase the number of steps in each sequence. When the dog remains close for 20 yards of straight-line heeling, it is time to add a few turns and then sign up for a happy-heeling obedience class to get some advice from the experts.

4) Use hand signal only to lure dog to sit as you stop. Eventually, dog will sit automatically at heel whenever you stop. 5) "Good dog!"

NO PULLING ON LEASH

You can start teaching your dog not to pull on leash anywhere—in front of the television or outdoors—but regardless of location, you must not take a single step with tension in the leash. For a reason known only to dogs, even just a couple of paces of pulling on leash is intrinsically motivating and diabolically rewarding. Instead, attach the leash to the dog's collar, grasp the other end firmly with both hands held close to your chest, and stand still—do not budge an inch. Have somebody watch you with a stopwatch to time your progress, or else you will never believe this will work and so you will not even try the exercise, and your shoulder and the dog's neck will be traumatized for years to come.

Stand still and wait for the dog to stop pulling, and to sit and/or lie down. All dogs stop pulling and sit eventually. Most take only a couple of minutes; the all-time record is 22 $\frac{1}{5}$ minutes. Time how long it takes. Gently praise the dog when he stops pulling, and as soon as he sits, enthusiastically praise the dog and take just one step forwards, then immediately stand still. This single step usually demonstrates the ballistic reinforcing nature of pulling on leash; most dogs explode to the end of the leash, so be prepared for the strain. Stand firm and wait for the dog to sit again. Repeat this half a dozen times and you will probably notice a progressive reduction in the force of the dog's one-step explosions and a radical reduction in the time it takes for the dog to sit each time.

As the dog learns "Sit we go" and "Pull we stop," she will begin to walk forward calmly with each single step and automatically sit when you stop. Now try two steps before you stop. Wooooooo! Scary! When the dog has mastered two steps at a time, try for three. After each success, progressively increase the number of steps in the sequence: try four steps and then six, eight, ten and twenty steps before stopping. Congratulations! You are now walking the dog on leash.

Whenever walking with the dog (off leash or on leash), make sure you stop periodically to practice a few position commands and stays before instructing the dog to "Walk on!" (Remember, you want the dog to be compliant everywhere, not just in the kitchen when his dinner is at hand.) For example, stopping every 25 yards to briefly train the dog amounts to over 200 training interludes within a single three-mile stroll. And each training session is in a different location. You will not believe the improvement within just the first mile of the first walk.

To put it another way, integrating training into a walk offers 200 separate opportunities to use the continuance of the walk as a reward to reinforce the dog's education. Moreover, some training interludes may comprise continuing education for the dog's walking skills: Alternate short periods of the dog walking calmly by your side with periods when the dog is allowed to sniff and investigate the environment. Now sniffing odors on the grass and meeting other dogs become rewards which reinforce the dog's calm and mannerly demeanor. Good Lord! Whatever next? Many enjoyable walks together of course. Happy trails!

THE IMPORTANCE OF TRICKS

Nothing will improve a dog's quality of life better than having a few tricks under its belt. Teaching any trick expands the dog's vocabulary, which facilitates communication and improves the owner's control. Also, specific tricks help prevent and resolve specific behavior problems. For example, by teaching the dog to fetch his toys, the dog learns carrying a toy makes the owner happy and, therefore, will be more likely to chew his toy than other inappropriate items.

More important, teaching tricks prompts owners to lighten up and train with a sunny disposition. Really, tricks should be no different from any other behaviors we put on cue. But they are. When teaching tricks, owners have a much sweeter attitude, which in turn motivates the dog and improves her willingness to comply. The dog feels tricks are a blast, but formal commands are a drag. In fact, tricks are so enjoyable, they may be used as rewards in training by asking the dog to come, sit and down-stay and then rollover for a tummy rub. Go on, try it: Crack a smile and even giggle when the dog promptly and willingly lies down and stays.

Most important, performing tricks prompts onlookers to smile and giggle. Many people are scared of dogs, especially large ones. And nothing can be more off-putting for a dog than to be constantly confronted by strangers who don't like him because of his size or the way he looks. Uneasy people put the dog on edge, causing him to back off and bark, only frightening people all the more. And so a vicious circle develops, with the people's fear fueling the dog's fear *and vice versa.* Instead, tie a pink ribbon to your dog's collar and practice all sorts of tricks on walks and in the park, and you will be pleasantly amazed how it changes people's attitudes toward your friendly dog. The dog's repertoire of tricks is limited only by the trainer's imagination. Below I have described three of my favorites:

SPEAK AND SHUSH

The training sequence involved in teaching a dog to bark on request is no different from that used when training any behavior on cue: request—lure—response—reward. As always, the secret of success lies in finding an effective lure. If the dog always barks at the doorbell, for example, say "Rover, speak!", have an accomplice ring the doorbell, then reward the dog for barking. After a few woofs, ask Rover to "Shush!", waggle a food treat under his nose (to entice him to sniff and thus to shush), praise him when quiet and eventually offer the treat as a reward. Alternate "Speak" and "Shush," progressively increasing the length of shush-time between each barking bout.

PLAYBOW

With the dog standing, say "Bow!" and lower the food lure (palm upwards) to rest between the dog's forepaws. Praise as the dog lowers

her forequarters and sternum to the ground (as when teaching the down), but then lure the dog to stand and offer the treat. On successive trials, gradually increase the length of time the dog is required to remain in the playbow posture in order to gain a food reward. If the dog's rear end collapses into a down, say nothing and offer no reward; simply start over.

BE A BEAR

With the dog sitting backed into a corner to prevent him from toppling over backwards, say "Be a Bear!" With bent paw and palm down, raise a lure upwards and backwards along the top of the dog's muzzle. Praise the dog when he sits up on his haunches and offer the treat as a reward. To prevent the dog from standing on his hind legs, keep the lure closer to the dog's muzzle. On each trial, progressively increase the length of time the dog is required to sit up to receive a food reward. Since lure/ reward training is so easy, teach the dog to stand and walk on his hind legs as well!

Teaching "Be a Bear"

chapter 9

Getting
Active
with your Dog

by Bardi McLennan

Once you and your dog have graduated from basic obedience training and are beginning to work together as a team, you can take part in the growing world of dog activities. There are so many fun things to do with your dog! Just remember, people and dogs don't always learn at the same pace, so don't be upset if you (or your dog) need more than two basic training courses before your team becomes operational. Even smart dogs don't go straight to college from kindergarten!

Just as there are events geared to certain types of dogs, so there are ones that are more appealing to certain types of people. In some activities, you give the commands and your dog does the work (upland game hunting is one example), while in others, such as agility, you'll both get a workout. You may want to aim for prestigious titles to add to your dog's name, or you may want nothing more than the sheer enjoyment of being around other people and their dogs. Passive or active, participation has its own rewards.

Consider your dog's physical capabilities when looking into any of the canine activities. It's easy to see that a Basset Hound is not built for the racetrack, nor would a Chihuahua be the breed of choice for pulling a sled. A loyal dog will attempt almost anything you ask him to do, so it is up to you to know your dog's limitations. A dog must be physically sound in order to compete at any level in athletic activities, and being mentally sound is a definite plus. Advanced age, however, may not be a deterrent. Many dogs still hunt and herd at ten or twelve years of age. It's entirely possible for dogs to be "fit at 50." Take your dog for a checkup, explain to your vet the type of activity you have in mind and be guided by his or her findings.

All dogs seem to love playing flyball.

You needn't be restricted to breed-specific sports if it's only fun you're after. Certain AKC activities are limited to designated breeds; however, as each new trial, test or sport has grown in popularity, so has the variety of breeds encouraged to participate at a fun level.

But don't shortchange your fun, or that of your dog, by thinking only of the basic function of her breed. Once a dog has learned how to learn, she can be taught to do just about anything as long as the size of the dog is right for the job and you both think it is fun and rewarding. In other words, you are a team.

To get involved in any of the activities detailed in this chapter, look for the names and addresses of the organizations that sponsor them in Chapter 13. You can also ask your breeder or a local dog trainer for contacts.

You can compete in obedience trials with a well trained dog.

Official American Kennel Club Activities

The following tests and trials are some of the events sanctioned by the AKC and sponsored by various dog clubs. Your dog's expertise will be rewarded with impressive titles. You can participate just for fun, or be competitive and go for those awards.

OBEDIENCE

Training classes begin with pups as young as three months of age in kindergarten puppy training, then advance to pre-novice (all exercises on lead) and go on to novice, which is where you'll start off-lead work. In obedience classes dogs learn to sit, stay, heel and come through a variety of exercises. Once you've got the basics down, you can enter obedience trials and work toward earning your dog's first degree, a C.D. (Companion Dog).

The next level is called "Open," in which jumps and retrieves perk up the dog's interest. Passing grades in competition at this level earn a C.D.X. (Companion Dog Excellent). Beyond that lies the goal of the most ambitious—Utility (U.D. and even U.D.X. or OTCh, an Obedience Champion).

AGILITY

All dogs can participate in the latest canine sport to have gained worldwide popularity for its fun and excitement, agility. It began in England as a canine version of horse show-jumping, but because dogs are more agile and able to perform on verbal commands, extra feats were added such as climbing, balancing and racing through tunnels or in and out of weave poles. Many of the obstacles (regulation or homemade) can be set up in your own backyard. If the agility bug bites, you could end up in international competition!

For starters, your dog should be obedience trained, even though, in the beginning, the lessons may all be taught on lead. Once the dog understands the commands (and you do, too), it's as easy as guiding the dog over a prescribed course, one obstacle at a time. In competition, the race is against the clock, so wear your running shoes! The dog starts with 200 points and the judge deducts for infractions and misadventures along the way.

All dogs seem to love agility and respond to it as if they were being turned loose in a playground paradise. Your dog's enthusiasm will be contagious; agility turns into great fun for dog and owner.

FIELD TRIALS AND HUNTING TESTS

There are field trials and hunting tests for the sporting breeds—retrievers, spaniels and pointing breeds, and for some hounds—Bassets, Beagles and Dachshunds. Field trials are competitive events that test a dog's ability to perform the functions for which she was bred. Hunting tests, which are open to retrievers,

---

TITLES AWARDED BY THE AKC

Conformation: Ch. (Champion)

Obedience: CD (Companion Dog); CDX (Companion Dog Excellent); UD (Utility Dog); UDX (Utility Dog Excellent); OTCh. (Obedience Trial Champion)

Field: JH (Junior Hunter); SH (Senior Hunter); MH (Master Hunter); AFCh. (Amateur Field Champion); FCh. (Field Champion)

Lure Coursing: JC (Junior Courser); SC (Senior Courser)

Herding: HT (Herding Tested); PT (Pre-Trial Tested); HS (Herding Started); HI (Herding Intermediate); HX (Herding Excellent); HCh. (Herding Champion)

Tracking: TD (Tracking Dog); TDX (Tracking Dog Excellent)

Agility: NAD (Novice Agility); OAD (Open Agility); ADX (Agility Excellent); MAX (Master Agility)

Earthdog Tests: JE (Junior Earthdog); SE (Senior Earthdog); ME (Master Earthdog)

Canine Good Citizen: CGC

Combination: DC (Dual Champion—Ch. and Fch.); TC (Triple Champion—Ch., Fch., and OTCh.)

spaniels and pointing breeds only, are noncompetitive and are a means of judging the dog's ability as well as that of the handler.

Hunting is a very large and complex part of canine sports, and if you own one of the breeds that hunts, the events are a great treat for your dog and you. He gets to do what he was bred for, and you get to work with him and watch him do it. You'll be proud of and amazed at what your dog can do.

Fortunately, the AKC publishes a series of booklets on these events, which outline the rules and regulations and include a glossary of the sometimes complicated terms. The AKC also publishes newsletters for field trialers and hunting test enthusiasts. The United Kennel Club (UKC) also has informative materials for the hunter and his dog.

Retrievers and other sporting breeds get to do what they're bred to in hunting tests.

HERDING TESTS AND TRIALS

Herding, like hunting, dates back to the first known uses man made of dogs. The interest in herding today is widespread, and if you own a herding breed, you can join in the activity. Herding dogs are tested for their natural skills to keep a flock of ducks, sheep or cattle together. If your dog shows potential, you can start at the testing level, where your dog can earn a title for showing an inherent herding ability. With training you can advance to the trial level, where your dog should be capable of controlling even difficult livestock in diverse situations.

LURE COURSING

The AKC Tests and Trials for Lure Coursing are open to traditional sighthounds—Greyhounds, Whippets,

Borzoi, Salukis, Afghan Hounds, Ibizan Hounds and Scottish Deerhounds—as well as to Basenjis and Rhodesian Ridgebacks. Hounds are judged on overall ability, follow, speed, agility and endurance. This is possibly the most exciting of the trials for spectators, because the speed and agility of the dogs is awesome to watch as they chase the lure (or "course") in heats of two or three dogs at a time.

TRACKING

Tracking is another activity in which almost any dog can compete because every dog that sniffs the ground when taken outdoors is, in fact, tracking. The hard part comes when the rules as to what, when and where the dog tracks are determined by a person, not the dog! Tracking tests cover a large area of fields, woods and roads. The tracks are laid hours before the dogs go to work on them, and include "tricks" like cross-tracks and sharp turns. If you're interested in search-and-rescue work, this is the place to start.

This tracking dog is hot on the trail.

EARTHDOG TESTS FOR SMALL TERRIERS AND DACHSHUNDS

These tests are open to Australian, Bedlington, Border, Cairn, Dandie Dinmont, Smooth and Wire Fox, Lakeland, Norfolk, Norwich, Scottish, Sealyham, Skye, Welsh and West Highland White Terriers as well as Dachshunds. The dogs need no prior training for this terrier sport. There is a qualifying test on the day of the event, so dog and handler learn the rules on the spot. These tests, or "digs," sometimes end with informal races in the late afternoon.

Here are some of the extracurricular obedience and
racing activities that are not regulated by the AKC or
UKC, but are generally run by clubs or a group of dog
fanciers and are often open to all.

Canine Freestyle This activity is something new on
the scene and is variously likened to dancing, dressage
or ice skating. It is meant to show the athleticism of the
dog, but also requires showmanship on the part of the
dog's handler. If you and your dog like to ham it up for
friends, you might want to look into freestyle.

*Lure coursing
lets sighthounds
do what they do
best—run!*

Scent Hurdle Racing Scent hurdle racing is purely a
fun activity sponsored by obedience clubs with members forming competing teams. The height of the hurdles is based on the size of the shortest dog on the
team. On a signal, one team dog is released on each of
two side-by-side courses and must clear every hurdle
before picking up its own dumbbell from a platform
and returning over the jumps to the handler. As each
dog returns, the next on that team is sent. Of course,
that is what the dogs are supposed to do. When the
dogs improvise (going under or around the hurdles,
stealing another dog's dumbbell, and so forth), it no
doubt frustrates the handlers, but just adds to the fun
for everyone else.

Flyball This type of racing is similar, but after negoti-
ating the four hurdles, the dog comes to a flyball box,
steps on a lever that releases a tennis ball into the air,

catches the ball and returns over the hurdles to the starting point. This game also becomes extremely fun for spectators because the dogs sometimes cheat by catching a ball released by the dog in the next lane. Three titles can be earned—Flyball Dog (F.D.), Flyball Dog Excellent (F.D.X.) and Flyball Dog Champion (Fb.D.Ch.)—all awarded by the North American Flyball Association, Inc.

Dogsledding The name conjures up the Rocky Mountains or the frigid North, but you can find dogsled clubs in such unlikely spots as Maryland, North Carolina and Virginia! Dogsledding is primarily for the Nordic breeds such as the Alaskan Malamutes, Siberian Huskies and Samoyeds, but other breeds can try. There are some practical backyard applications to this sport, too. With parental supervision, almost any strong dog could pull a child's sled.

Coming over the A-frame on an agility course.

These are just some of the many recreational ways you can get to know and understand your multifaceted dog better and have fun doing it.

chapter 10

Your Dog
and your
Family

by Bardi McLennan

Adding a dog automatically increases your family by one, no matter whether you live alone in an apartment or are part of a mother, father and six kids household. The single-person family is fair game for numerous and varied canine misconceptions as to who is dog and who pays the bills, whereas a dog in a houseful of children will consider himself to be just one of the gang, littermates all. One dog and one child may give a dog reason to believe they are both kids or both dogs.

Either interpretation requires parental supervision and sometimes speedy intervention.

As soon as one paw goes through the door into your home, Rufus (or Rufina) has to make many adjustments to become a part of your family. Your job is to make him fit in as painlessly as possible. An older dog may have some frame of reference from past experience, but to a 10-week-old puppy, everything is brand new: people, furniture, stairs, when and where people eat, sleep or watch TV, his own place and everyone else's space, smells, sounds, outdoors—everything!

Puppies, and newly acquired dogs of any age, do not need what we think of as "freedom." If you leave a new dog or puppy loose in the house, you will almost certainly return to chaotic destruction and the dog will forever after equate your homecoming with a time of punishment to be dreaded. It is unfair to give your dog what amounts to "freedom to get into trouble." Instead, confine him to a crate for brief periods of your absence (up to three or four hours) and, for the long haul, a workday for example, confine him to one untrashable area with his own toys, a bowl of water and a radio left on (low) in another room.

Lots of pets get along with each other just fine.

For the first few days, when not confined, put Rufus on a long leash tied to your wrist or waist. This umbilical cord method enables the dog to learn all about you from your body language and voice, and to learn by his own actions which things in the house are NO! and which ones are rewarded by "Good dog." House-training will be easier with the pup always by your side. Speaking of which, accidents do happen. That goal of "completely housetrained" takes up to a year, or the length of time it takes the pup to mature.

The All-Adult Family

Most dogs in an adults-only household today are likely to be latchkey pets, with no one home all day but the dog. When you return after a tough day on the job, the dog can and should be your relaxation therapy. But going home can instead be a daily frustration.

Separation anxiety is a very common problem for the dog in a working household. It may begin with whines and barks of loneliness, but it will soon escalate into a frenzied destruction derby. That is why it is so important to set aside the time to teach a dog to relax when left alone in his confined area and to understand that he can trust you to return.

Let the dog get used to your work schedule in easy stages. Confine him to one room and go in and out of that room over and over again. Be casual about it. No physical, voice or eye contact. When the pup no longer even notices your comings and goings, leave the house for varying lengths of time, returning to stay home for a few minutes and gradually increasing the time away. This training can take days, but the dog is learning that you haven't left him forever and that he can trust you.

Any time you leave the dog, but especially during this training period, be casual about your departure. No anxiety-building fond farewells. Just "Bye" and go! Remember the "Good dog" when you return to find everything more or less as you left it.

If things are a mess (or even a disaster) when you return, greet the dog, take him outside to eliminate, and then put him in his crate while you clean up. Rant and rave in the shower! *Do not* punish the dog. You were not there when it happened, and the rule is: Only punish as you catch the dog in the act of wrongdoing. Obviously, it makes sense to get your latchkey puppy when you'll have a week or two to spend on these training essentials.

Family weekend activities should include Rufus whenever possible. Depending on the pup's age, now is the time for a long walk in the park, playtime in the backyard, a hike in the woods. Socializing is as important as health care, good food and physical exercise, so visiting Aunt Emma or Uncle Harry and the next-door neighbor's dog or cat is essential to developing an outgoing, friendly temperament in your pet.

If you are a single adult, socializing Rufus at home and away will prevent him from becoming overly protective of you (or just overly attached) and will also prevent such behavioral problems as dominance or fear of strangers.

Babies

Whether already here or on the way, babies figure larger than life in the eyes of a dog. If the dog is there first, let him in on all your baby preparations in the house. When baby arrives, let Rufus sniff any item of clothing that has been on the baby before Junior comes home. Then let Mom greet the dog first before introducing the new family member. Hold the baby down for the dog to see and sniff, but make sure someone's holding the dog on lead in case of any sudden moves. Don't play keep-away or tease the dog with the baby, which only invites undesirable jumping up.

The dog and the baby are "family," and for starters can be treated almost as equals. Things rapidly change, however, especially when baby takes to creeping around on all fours on the dog's turf or, better yet, has yummy pudding all over her face and hands! That's when a lot of things in the dog's and baby's lives become more separate than equal.

Dogs are perfect confidants.

Toddlers make terrible dog owners, but if you can't avoid the combination, use patient discipline (that is, positive teaching rather than punishment), and use time-outs before you run out of patience.

139

A dog and a baby (or toddler, or an assertive young child) should never be left alone together. Take the dog with you or confine him. With a baby or youngsters in the house, you'll have plenty of use for that wonderful canine safety device called a crate!

Young Children

Any dog in a house with kids will behave pretty much as the kids do, good or bad. But even good dogs and good children can get into trouble when play becomes rowdy and active.

Legs bobbing up and down, shrill voices screeching, a ball hurtling overhead, all add up to exuberant frustration for a dog who's just trying to be part of the gang. In a pack of puppies, any legs or toys being chased would be caught by a set of teeth, and all the pups involved would understand that is how the game is played. Kids do not understand this, nor do parents tolerate it. Bring Rufus indoors before you have reason to regret it. This is time-out, not a punishment.

Teach children how to play nicely with a puppy.

You can explain the situation to the children and tell them they must play quieter games until the puppy learns not to grab them with his mouth. Unfortunately, you can't explain it that easily to the dog. With adult supervision, they will learn how to play together.

Young children love to tease. Sticking their faces or wiggling their hands or fingers in the dog's face is teasing. To another person it might be just annoying, but it is threatening to a dog. There's another difference: We can make the child stop by an explanation, but the only way a dog can stop it is with a warning growl and then with teeth. Teasing is the major cause of children being bitten by their pets. Treat it seriously.

Older Children

The best age for a child to get a first dog is between the ages of 8 and 12. That's when kids are able to accept some real responsibility for their pet. Even so, take the child's vow of "I will never *ever* forget to feed (brush, walk, etc.) the dog" for what it's worth: a child's good intention at that moment. Most kids today have extra lessons, soccer practice, Little League, ballet, and so forth piled on top of school schedules. There will be many times when Mom will have to come to the dog's rescue. "I walked the dog for you so you can set the table for me" is one way to get around a missed appointment without laying on blame or guilt.

Kids in this age group make excellent obedience trainers because they are into the teaching/learning process themselves and they lack the self-consciousness of adults. Attending a dog show is something the whole family can enjoy, and watching Junior Showmanship may catch the eye of the kids. Older children can begin to get involved in many of the recreational activities that were reviewed in the previous chapter. Some of the agility obstacles, for example, can be set up in the backyard as a family project (with an adult making sure all the equipment is safe and secure for the dog).

Older kids are also beginning to look to the future, and may envision themselves as veterinarians or trainers or show dog handlers or writers of the next Lassie best-seller. Dogs are perfect confidants for these dreams. They won't tell a soul.

Other Pets

Introduce all pets tactfully. In a dog/cat situation, hold the dog, not the cat. Let two dogs meet on neutral turf—a stroll in the park or a walk down the street—with both on loose leads to permit all the normal canine ways of saying hello, including routine sniffing, circling, more sniffing, and so on. Small creatures such as hamsters, chinchillas or mice must be kept safe from their natural predators (dogs and cats).

Festive Family Occasions

Parties are great for people, but not necessarily for puppies. Until all the guests have arrived, put the dog in his crate or in a room where he won't be disturbed. A socialized dog can join the fun later as long as he's not underfoot, annoying guests or into the hors d'oeuvres.

There are a few dangers to consider, too. Doors opening and closing can allow a puppy to slip out unnoticed in the confusion, and you'll be organizing a search party instead of playing host or hostess. Party food and buffet service are not for dogs. Let Rufus party in his crate with a nice big dog biscuit.

At Christmas time, not only are tree decorations dangerous and breakable (and perhaps family heirlooms), but extreme caution should be taken with the lights, cords and outlets for the tree lights and any other festive lighting. Occasionally a dog lifts a leg, ignoring the fact that the tree is indoors. To avoid this, use a canine repellent, made for gardens, on the tree. Or keep him out of the tree room unless supervised. And whatever you do, *don't* invite trouble by hanging his toys on the tree!

Car Travel

Before you plan a vacation by car or RV with Rufus, be sure he enjoys car travel. Nothing spoils a holiday quicker than a carsick dog! Work within the dog's comfort level. Get in the car with the dog in his crate or attached to a canine car safety belt and just sit there until he relaxes. That's all. Next time, get in the car, turn on the engine and go nowhere. Just sit. When that is okay, turn on the engine and go around the block. Now you can go for a ride and include a stop where you get out, leaving the dog for a minute or two.

On a warm day, always park in the shade and leave windows open several inches. And return quickly. It only takes 10 minutes for a car to become an overheated steel death trap.

Motel or Pet Motel?

Not all motels or hotels accept pets, but you have a much better choice today than even a few years ago. To find a dog-friendly lodging, look at *On the Road Again With Man's Best Friend*, a series of directories that detail bed and breakfasts, inns, family resorts and other hotels/motels. Some places require a refundable deposit to cover any damage incurred by the dog. More B&Bs accept pets now, but some restrict the size.

If taking Rufus with you is not feasible, check out boarding kennels in your area. Your veterinarian may offer this service, or recommend a kennel or two he or she is familiar with. Go see the facilities for yourself, ask about exercise, diet, housing, and so on. Or, if you'd rather have Rufus stay home, look into bonded petsitters, many of whom will also bring in the mail and water your plants.

11

Your Dog
and your
Community

by Bardi McLennan

Step outside your home with your dog and you are no longer just family, you are both part of your community. This is when the phrase "responsible pet ownership" takes on serious implications. For starters, it means you pick up after your dog—not just occasionally, but every time your dog eliminates away from home. That means you have joined the Plastic Baggy Brigade! You always have plastic sandwich bags in your pocket and several in the car. It means you teach your kids how to use them, too. If you think this is "yucky," just imagine what

the person (a non-doggy person) who inadvertently steps in the mess thinks!

Your responsibility extends to your neighbors: To their ears (no annoying barking); to their property (their garbage, their lawn, their flower beds, their cat—especially their cat); to their kids (on bikes, at play); to their kids' toys and sports equipment.

There are numerous dog-related laws, ranging from simple dog licensing and leash laws to those holding you liable for any physical injury or property damage done by your dog. These laws are in place to protect everyone in the community, including you and your dog. There are town ordinances and state laws which are by no means the same in all towns or all states. Ignorance of the law won't get you off the hook. The time to find out what the laws are where you live is now.

Be sure your dog's license is current. This is not just a good local ordinance, it can make the difference between finding your lost dog or not.

Dressing your dog up makes him appealing to strangers.

Many states now require proof of rabies vaccination and that the dog has been spayed or neutered before issuing a license. At the same time, keep up the dog's annual immunizations.

Never let your dog run loose in the neighborhood. This will not only keep you on the right side of the leash law, it's the outdoor version of the rule about not giving your dog "freedom to get into trouble."

Good Canine Citizen

Sometimes it's hard for a dog's owner to assess whether or not the dog is sufficiently socialized to be accepted by the community at large. Does Rufus or Rufina display good, controlled behavior in public? The AKC's Canine Good Citizen program is available through many dog organizations. If your dog passes the test, the title "CGC" is earned.

The overall purpose is to turn your dog into a good neighbor and to teach you about your responsibility to your community as a dog owner. Here are the ten things your dog must do willingly:

1. Accept a stranger stopping to chat with you.
2. Sit and be petted by a stranger.
3. Allow a stranger to handle him or her as a groomer or veterinarian would.
4. Walk nicely on a loose lead.
5. Walk calmly through a crowd.
6. Sit and down on command, then stay in a sit or down position while you walk away.
7. Come when called.
8. Casually greet another dog.
9. React confidently to distractions.
10. Accept being left alone with someone other than you and not become overly agitated or nervous.

Schools and Dogs

Schools are getting involved with pet ownership on an educational level. It has been proven that children who are kind to animals are humane in their attitude toward other people as adults.

A dog is a child's best friend, and so children are often primary pet owners, if not the primary caregivers. Unfortunately, they are also the ones most often bitten by dogs. This occurs due to a lack of understanding that pets, no matter how sweet, cuddly and loving, are still animals. Schools, along with parents, dog clubs, dog fanciers and the AKC, are working to change all that with video programs for children not only in grade school, but in the nursery school and pre-kindergarten age group. Teaching youngsters how to be responsible dog owners is important community work. When your dog has a CGC, volunteer to take part in an educational classroom event put on by your dog club.

Boy Scout Merit Badge

A Merit Badge for Dog Care can be earned by any Boy Scout ages 11 to 18. The requirements are not easy, but amount to a complete course in responsible dog care and general ownership. Here are just a few of the things a Scout must do to earn that badge:

> Point out ten parts of the dog using the correct names.

> Give a report (signed by parent or guardian) on your care of the dog (feeding, food used, housing, exercising, grooming and bathing), plus what has been done to keep the dog healthy.

> Explain the right way to obedience train a dog, and demonstrate three comments.

> Several of the requirements have to do with health care, including first aid, handling a hurt dog, and the dangers of home treatment for a serious ailment.

> The final requirement is to know the local laws and ordinances involving dogs.

There are similar programs for Girl Scouts and 4-H members.

Local Clubs

Local dog clubs are no longer in existence just to put on a yearly dog show. Today, they are apt to be the hub of the community's involvement with pets. Dog clubs conduct educational forums with big-name speakers, stage demonstrations of canine talent in a busy mall and take dogs of various breeds to schools for classroom discussion.

The quickest way to feel accepted as a member in a club is to volunteer your services! Offer to help with something—anything—and watch your popularity (and your interest) grow.

Therapy Dogs

Once your dog has earned that essential CGC and reliably demonstrates a steady, calm temperament, you could look into what therapy dogs are doing in your area.

Therapy dogs go with their owners to visit patients at hospitals or nursing homes, generally remaining on leash but able to coax a pat from a stiffened hand, a smile from a blank face, a few words from sealed lips or a hug from someone in need of love.

Nursing homes cover a wide range of patient care. Some specialize in care of the elderly, some in the treatment of specific illnesses, some in physical therapy. Children's facilities also welcome visits from trained therapy dogs for boosting morale in their pediatric patients. Hospice care for the terminally ill and the at-home care of AIDS patients are other areas where this canine visiting is desperately needed. Therapy dog training comes first.

Your dog can make a difference in lots of lives.

There is a lot more involved than just taking your nice friendly pooch to someone's bedside. Doing therapy dog work involves your own emotional stability as well as that of your dog. But once you have met all the requirements for this work, making the rounds once a week or once a month with your therapy dog is possibly the most rewarding of all community activities.

Disaster Aid

This community service is definitely not for everyone, partly because it is time-consuming. The initial training is rigorous, and there can be no let-up in the continuing workouts, because members are on call 24 hours a day to go wherever they are needed at a moment's notice. But if you think you would like to be able to assist in a disaster, look into search-and-rescue work. The network of search-and-rescue volunteers is worldwide, and all members of the American Rescue Dog Association (ARDA) who are qualified to do this work are volunteers who train and maintain their own dogs.

Physical Aid

Most people are familiar with Seeing Eye dogs, which serve as blind people's eyes, but not with all the other work that dogs are trained to do to assist the disabled. Dogs are also specially trained to pull wheelchairs, carry school books, pick up dropped objects, open and close doors. Some also are ears for the deaf. All these assistance-trained dogs, by the way, are allowed anywhere "No Pet" signs exist (as are therapy dogs when properly identified). Getting started in any of this fascinating work requires a background in dog training and canine behavior, but there are also volunteer jobs ranging from answering the phone to cleaning out kennels to providing a foster home for a puppy. You have only to ask.

Making the rounds with your therapy dog can be very rewarding.

part four

Beyond the Basics

Recommended Reading

Books

ABOUT HEALTH CARE

Ackerman, Lowell. *Guide to Skin and Haircoat Problems in Dogs.* Loveland, Colo.: Alpine Publications, 1994.

Alderton, David. *The Dog Care Manual.* Hauppauge, N.Y.: Barron's Educational Series, Inc., 1986.

American Kennel Club. *American Kennel Club Dog Care and Training.* New York: Howell Book House, 1991.

Bamberger, Michelle, DVM. *Help! The Quick Guide to First Aid for Your Dog.* New York: Howell Book House, 1995.

Carlson, Delbert, DVM, and James Giffin, MD. *Dog Owner's Home Veterinary Handbook.* New York: Howell Book House, 1992.

DeBitetto, James, DVM, and Sarah Hodgson. *You & Your Puppy.* New York: Howell Book House, 1995.

Humphries, Jim, DVM. *Dr. Jim's Animal Clinic for Dogs.* New York: Howell Book House, 1994.

McGinnis, Terri. *The Well Dog Book.* New York: Random House, 1991.

Pitcairn, Richard and Susan. *Natural Health for Dogs.* Emmaus, Pa.: Rodale Press, 1982.

ABOUT DOG SHOWS

Hall, Lynn. *Dog Showing for Beginners.* New York: Howell Book House, 1994.

Nichols, Virginia Tuck. *How to Show Your Own Dog.* Neptune, N. J.: TFH, 1970.

Vanacore, Connie. *Dog Showing, An Owner's Guide.* New York: Howell Book House, 1990.

ABOUT TRAINING

Ammen, Amy. *Training in No Time*. New York: Howell Book House, 1995.

Baer, Ted. *Communicating With Your Dog*. Hauppauge, N.Y.: Barron's Educational Series, Inc., 1989.

Benjamin, Carol Lea. *Dog Problems*. New York: Howell Book House, 1989.

Benjamin, Carol Lea. *Dog Training for Kids*. New York: Howell Book House, 1988.

Benjamin, Carol Lea. *Mother Knows Best*. New York: Howell Book House, 1985.

Benjamin, Carol Lea. *Surviving Your Dog's Adolescence*. New York: Howell Book House, 1993.

Bohnenkamp, Gwen. *Manners for the Modern Dog*. San Francisco: Perfect Paws, 1990.

Dibra, Bashkim. *Dog Training by Bash*. New York: Dell, 1992.

Dunbar, Ian, PhD, MRCVS. *Dr. Dunbar's Good Little Dog Book*, James & Kenneth Publishers, 2140 Shattuck Ave. #2406, Berkeley, Calif. 94704. (510) 658–8588. Order from the publisher.

Dunbar, Ian, PhD, MRCVS. *How to Teach a New Dog Old Tricks*, James & Kenneth Publishers. Order from the publisher; address above.

Dunbar, Ian, PhD, MRCVS, and Gwen Bohnenkamp. Booklets on *Preventing Aggression; Housetraining; Chewing; Digging; Barking; Socialization; Fearfulness; and Fighting*, James & Kenneth Publishers. Order from the publisher; address above.

Evans, Job Michael. *People, Pooches and Problems*. New York: Howell Book House, 1991.

Kilcommons, Brian and Sarah Wilson. *Good Owners, Great Dogs*. New York: Warner Books, 1992.

McMains, Joel M. *Dog Logic—Companion Obedience*. New York: Howell Book House, 1992.

Rutherford, Clarice and David H. Neil, MRCVS. *How to Raise a Puppy You Can Live With*. Loveland, Colo.: Alpine Publications, 1982.

Volhard, Jack and Melissa Bartlett. *What All Good Dogs Should Know: The Sensible Way to Train*. New York: Howell Book House, 1991.

ABOUT BREEDING

Harris, Beth J. Finder. *Breeding a Litter, The Complete Book of Prenatal and Postnatal Care*. New York: Howell Book House, 1983.

Holst, Phyllis, DVM. *Canine Reproduction*. Loveland, Colo.: Alpine Publications, 1985.

Walkowicz, Chris and Bonnie Wilcox, DVM. *Successful Dog Breeding, The Complete Handbook of Canine Midwifery.* New York: Howell Book House, 1994.

ABOUT ACTIVITIES

American Rescue Dog Association. *Search and Rescue Dogs.* New York: Howell Book House, 1991.

Barwig, Susan and Stewart Hilliard. *Schutzhund.* New York: Howell Book House, 1991.

Beaman, Arthur S. *Lure Coursing.* New York: Howell Book House, 1994.

Daniels, Julie. *Enjoying Dog Agility—From Backyard to Competition.* New York: Doral Publishing, 1990.

Davis, Kathy Diamond. *Therapy Dogs.* New York: Howell Book House, 1992.

Gallup, Davis Anne. *Running With Man's Best Friend.* Loveland, Colo.: Alpine Publications, 1986.

Habgood, Dawn and Robert. *On the Road Again With Man's Best Friend.* New England, Mid-Atlantic, West Coast and Southeast editions. Selective guides to area bed and breakfasts, inns, hotels and resorts that welcome guests and their dogs. New York: Howell Book House, 1995.

Holland, Vergil S. *Herding Dogs.* New York: Howell Book House, 1994.

LaBelle, Charlene G. *Backpacking With Your Dog.* Loveland, Colo.: Alpine Publications, 1993.

Simmons-Moake, Jane. *Agility Training, The Fun Sport for All Dogs.* New York: Howell Book House, 1991.

Spencer, James B. *Hup! Training Flushing Spaniels the American Way.* New York: Howell Book House, 1992.

Spencer, James B. *Point! Training the All-Seasons Birddog.* New York: Howell Book House, 1995.

Tarrant, Bill. *Training the Hunting Retriever.* New York: Howell Book House, 1991.

Volhard, Jack and Wendy. *The Canine Good Citizen.* New York: Howell Book House, 1994.

General Titles

Haggerty, Captain Arthur J. *How to Get Your Pet Into Show Business.* New York: Howell Book House, 1994.

McLennan, Bardi. *Dogs and Kids, Parenting Tips.* New York: Howell Book House, 1993.

Moran, Patti J. *Pet Sitting for Profit, A Complete Manual for Professional Success.* New York: Howell Book House, 1992.

Scalisi, Danny and Libby Moses. *When Rover Just Won't Do, Over 2,000 Suggestions for Naming Your Dog.* New York: Howell Book House, 1993.

Sife, Wallace, PhD. *The Loss of a Pet.* New York: Howell Book House, 1993.

Wrede, Barbara J. *Civilizing Your Puppy.* Hauppauge, N.Y.: Barron's Educational Series, 1992.

Magazines

The AKC GAZETTE, The Official Journal for the Sport of Purebred Dogs. American Kennel Club, 51 Madison Ave., New York, NY.

Bloodlines Journal. United Kennel Club, 100 E. Kilgore Rd., Kalamazoo, MI.

Dog Fancy. Fancy Publications, 3 Burroughs, Irvine, CA 92718

Dog World. Maclean Hunter Publishing Corp., 29 N. Wacker Dr., Chicago, IL 60606.

Videos

"SIRIUS Puppy Training," by Ian Dunbar, PhD, MRCVS. James & Kenneth Publishers, 2140 Shattuck Ave. #2406, Berkeley, CA 94704. Order from the publisher.

"Training the Companion Dog," from Dr. Dunbar's British TV Series, James & Kenneth Publishers. (See address above).

The American Kennel Club produces videos on every breed of dog, as well as on hunting tests, field trials and other areas of interest to purebred dog owners. For more information, write to AKC/Video Fulfillment, 5580 Centerview Dr., Suite 200, Raleigh, NC 27606.

Resources

Breed Clubs

Every breed recognized by the American Kennel Club has a national (parent) club. National clubs are a great source of information on your breed. You can get the name of the secretary of the club by contacting:

The American Kennel Club
51 Madison Avenue
New York, NY 10010
(212) 696-8200

There are also numerous all-breed, individual breed, obedience, hunting and other special-interest dog clubs across the country. The American Kennel Club can provide you with a geographical list of clubs to find ones in your area. Contact them at the above address.

Registry Organizations

Registry organizations register purebred dogs. The American Kennel Club is the oldest and largest in this country, and currently recognizes over 130 breeds. The United Kennel Club registers some breeds the AKC doesn't (including the American Pit Bull Terrier and the Miniature Fox Terrier) as well as many of the same breeds. The others included here are for your reference; the AKC can provide you with a list of foreign registries.

American Kennel Club
51 Madison Avenue
New York, NY 10010

United Kennel Club (UKC)
100 E. Kilgore Road
Kalamazoo, MI 49001-5598

American Dog Breeders Assn.
P.O. Box 1771
Salt Lake City, UT 84110
(Registers American Pit Bull Terriers)

Canadian Kennel Club
89 Skyway Avenue
Etobicoke, Ontario
Canada M9W 6R4

National Stock Dog Registry
P.O. Box 402
Butler, IN 46721
(Registers working stock dogs)

Orthopedic Foundation for Animals (OFA)
2300 E. Nifong Blvd.
Columbia, MO 65201-3856
(Hip registry)

Activity Clubs

Write to these organizations for information on the
activities they sponsor.

American Kennel Club
51 Madison Avenue
New York, NY 10010
(Conformation Shows, Obedience Trials, Field
Trials and Hunting Tests, Agility, Canine Good

Citizen, Lure Coursing, Herding, Tracking,
Earthdog Tests, Coonhunting.)

United Kennel Club
100 E. Kilgore Road
Kalamazoo, MI 49001-5598
(Conformation Shows, Obedience Trials, Agility,
Hunting for Various Breeds, Terrier Trials and
more.)

North American Flyball Assn.
1342 Jeff St.
Ypsilanti, MI 48198

International Sled Dog Racing Assn.
P.O. Box 446
Norman, ID 83848-0446

North American Working Dog Assn., Inc.
Southeast Kreisgruppe
P.O. Box 833
Brunswick, GA 31521

Trainers

Association of Pet Dog Trainers
P.O. Box 3734
Salinas, CA 93912
(408) 663–9257

American Dog Trainers' Network
161 West 4th St.
New York, NY 10014
(212) 727–7257

**National Association of Dog Obedience
Instructors**
2286 East Steel Rd.
St. Johns, MI 48879

Associations

American Dog Owners Assn.
1654 Columbia Tpk.
Castleton, NY 12033
(Combats anti-dog legislation)

Delta Society
P.O. Box 1080
Renton, WA 98057-1080
(Promotes the human/animal bond through
pet-assisted therapy and other programs)

Dog Writers Assn. of America (DWAA)
Sally Cooper, Secy.
222 Woodchuck Ln.
Harwinton, CT 06791

National Assn. for Search and Rescue (NASAR)
P.O. Box 3709
Fairfax, VA 22038

Therapy Dogs International
6 Hilltop Road
Mendham, NJ 07945